THE ULTIMATE GUIDE TO NAVIGATING WITHOUT A COMPASS

THE ULTIMATE GUIDE TO NAVIGATING WITHOUT A COMPASS

How to Find Your Way Using the Sun, Stars, and Other Natural Methods

CHRISTOPHER NYERGES

Skyhorse Publishing

Skyhorse Publishing books may be purchased in bulk at special discounts for sales promotion, corporate gifts, fund-raising, or educational purposes. Special editions can also be created to specifications. For details, contact the Special Sales Department, Skyhorse Publishing, 307 West 36th Street, 11th Floor, New York, NY 10018 or info@skyhorsepublishing.com.

Visit our website at www.skyhorsepublishing.com.

10 9 8 7 6 5 4 3

Library of Congress Cataloging-in-Publication Data is available on file.

Cover design by Tom Lau
All photos courtesy of the author, unless otherwise noted

Print ISBN: 978-1-5107-4990-0
Ebook ISBN: 978-1-5107-4992-4

Printed in China

TABLE OF CONTENTS

ACKNOWLEDGMENTS

I've been trying to get somewhere all my life, and have always been interested in the concept of "direction" and how to accurately navigate from place to place. It's not as complicated as you might think, but it does take the constant paying of attention. I think I've compiled just about every tidbit about orienteering and natural navigation I've ever heard in this book, and it came from many sources.

In my early years, I loved the writings of Bradford Angier and Ellsworth Jaegar, as well as the more practical writings of Björn Kjellström. In the real world, I've learned much from my companions and associates, such as Ron Hood (of Survival.com), Abbey Keith (of the Sierra Madre Search and Rescue team), and my fellow members of Dirttime: Dude McLean, Alan Halcon, and John McCann. Halcon spent a considerable amount of his time assisting me in making this book as good as possible, given our constraints of time and space.

In the early days, Richard E. White encouraged me to learn how sundials and sun compasses work, and how to make them. My astronomy teacher at Pasadena City College, Mr. Eaton, taught me that so much of this is pure math—"You'll never get this if you don't grasp the math," he would tell us. I learned quickly when I was asked to teach how to use a map and compass through the WTI Survival Training School, and through Pasadena City College. Teaching demonstrates that you know, or you don't know, and I quickly learned what I *did not know*.

Even my father began my navigation training early, when he drilled into me how and where to walk home from kindergarten and grade school, with a specific pattern, and always observing the unexpected, so that "the boogeyman doesn't get you." I extend my gratitude to each of you who assisted me on this path.

INTRODUCTION

TIME AND DIRECTION

Natural navigation, and the observation of the sun, moon, and stars, is a complex process that also necessarily involves the concepts of time and time-keeping. Sundials and compasses are intimately related, for example. But our focus here is navigation, with or without a compass, and so we will address the motions of the earth, sun, moon, and stars as they pertain to navigation primarily, and as they relate to time-keeping only when necessary.

Ancient people did not have any of our modern technology, and so they developed an acute awareness of their environments, including the movement of the sun, the moon, and the stars. They knew where they were in relation to other things, and they developed unique tools for maintaining this sense of awareness.

Modern people rarely think about north vs. south, the divisions of time, or how these things are figured, adjusted, or corrected. Why? We've let our technological tools do this work for us, and as an unintended consequence, we've grown increasingly unaware and ignorant of our surroundings.

In this book, we hope to awaken in you that excitement that comes with learning how to determine north from the stars, how to determine east from the sun, and how to use your natural sense of awareness to guide you.

This book is an excellent first step towards developing those skills which will lead to a greater sense of direction—in the city, or in the woods.

Q: Is it true that you were once hopelessly lost in the woods?
A: No, but I was very confused for a few days.

"Remember, you're not lost. It's your camp that is lost."
—Ellsworth Jaeger

CHAPTER 1

NATURAL OBSERVATIONS

You want to go natural. You want to shed all vestiges of civilization and throw away your maps and compasses, and learn to live off the land and read the landscape like a native. Right?

How do you do so?

In fact, there is no *single* natural observation that will tell you directions. You need to be observant of many features and understand what they mean. You need to use your common sense and you need to be able to "think on your feet." Then, with practice, you stand a good chance of determining compass points and knowing how to get around without modern devices.

Here are a few of those general guidelines. Keep in mind that some would put these observations into the category of "folklore." This is because they are *general* guidelines. Rely on these alone and you may still remain hopelessly lost. In fact, I was once pompously informed that I should not teach any such navigation techniques if they are not foolproof and 100 percent accurate all the time. Really? Though the person who told me that probably had the best of intentions, I merely responded, "Welcome to the real world." In the real world that I have come to know, this world that we are going to learn to navigate, we need to blend subjectivity with objectivity, hard facts with intuition, pragmatism with pleasure, as well as the hard fact versus harsh realities.

Getting Yourself Oriented

Studying the Lay of the Land

The best way to understand the landscape you're in is to get to a high spot where you can observe as much of the local terrain as possible. Get up to a rocky peak, or some high area with an unimpeded view of the terrain. Once, when there was no such high spot, I actually climbed a tree in order to get a look at the lay of the land.

Look for the flat zones—where water flows, the high peaks, the undulating valleys—anything that relates to your ability to travel and to obtain water. If you have the ability to jot down in a notebook some

Observe your landscape, ideally from a high elevation. Binoculars can help you spot details.

of your observations, you should do so, especially if it's your first time in a new area.

Observing where water flows is important from a navigational standpoint because you might have to cross a body of water. You'll need to go around, or cross it where the river is either narrowest (where it would be easy to have a makeshift bridge), or where the river is widest (where the water is the most shallow). Also, there are often trails along a river or stream because they are often easy to follow, and easy to get to the next town or village downstream. (Remember, "often" is not synonymous with "always".)

A map is the most convenient and reliable way to study unknown landscapes, so you should get a map for the area you're in, and take advantage of all that it tells you. But if you don't have one, and can't get to high ground, there are still plenty of observations you should be making.

Always Look Back

As you travel, don't only look forward to the next turn in the road. If you know you'll be coming back the same way, you should make the habit of constantly looking back. Why? Is it because someone might be following you? No, not necessarily.

People have gotten lost on their return trips because they didn't recognize the terrain they had just walked through hours before! How is that possible? Just try it the next time you're on the trail. Hills and trees and bridges and trails and canyons looks very different from the opposite angle, often with a different light from later in the day.

Using Boulders

Boulders will absorb the heat from the sun during the day, and some campers have discovered that if they sleep near large boulders, they will stay warmer as the heat slowly radiates. Darker-colored boulders will absorb more heat than light-colored boulders.

If it's slightly after sundown, you might be able to determine north from south (roughly) by feeling large boulders. You'll feel more heat on the southern exposed sections than you will on the northern half. This all depends on the configuration of the boulder, of course, and how exposed it was to the sun.

Using Trees

Moss on Trees

You have no map, no compass, and you're lost or confused. Are there signs in nature to tell you directions?

We have long heard that moss grows on the north side of trees. We have all heard this so often, in so many formats, that you'd think it was some sort of absolute dogma. I still recall in my high school years when I was taking backpacking and survival classes from Abbey Keith of the Sierra Madre Search and Rescue Team. Keith liked to ask us a lot of questions.

This patch of moss was growing on the northwest side of the tree.

On one Saturday morning, he asked all of us, "Does moss grow on the north sides of trees?" The room was somewhat silent. Everyone was leaning towards a strong "yes," but no one answered. "Yes," said Keith loudly with a broad grin. "It does! But it also grows on the east side, the south side, and the west side of trees, especially in a dense forest where there is little light." Everyone laughed.

Though there is logic to this idea, and though in a clearing the moss is predominantly on the northern half of the tree (there's less light and more moisture there), it is not a precise, nor reliable, method of direction-finding. Keith would later tell us that *if* it's a pine tree, and *if* you're in California, and *if* the tree is in a clearing, then the moss is *probably* on the north half of the tree. Somewhat useful, but not very good for precision direction-finding.

Other Tree Observations

Another observation to take with trees is to place your palm onto the tree, and move your palm around the trunk. The general rule of thumb is that the tree is warmer on the south side, and cooler on the north side. I have tried this a lot, and found that though there is great variation among trees, there does seem to be a kernel of truth to this folk observation.

Collectors of spruce gum in the woods have pointed out that when the gum that oozes from the tree is a clear amber color, it's generally on the south side of the tree. If the gum is a dirty gray color, it's usually on the north side of the tree. *Hmmmm*?

If you encounter a tree stump that has been neatly cut, observe the tree rings. On some trees, under certain circumstances, you will note that the rings are wider towards the north and northeast. The bark might also be thicker on the north and northeastern sections. This might help in your natural orienteering, in addition to many other observations.

Tips of trees

Tips of certain trees will tend to point in specific directions. This is usually a result of prevailing local winds, and because the tree tips are the most tender and susceptible to bending.

These tall trees often sway in the wind. Discerning directions from them, however, can be difficult.

These tree tips will sway whatever way the wind is blowing. Sometimes, however, the tips will indicate the dominant wind direction.

Sometimes you can glean directions from trees, sometimes not. If you walk entirely around some trees, you might note thicker growth on one side.

The tops of willows, poplars, and alders often point south because they grow typically in canyons or streams, which are (more often than not), flowing southward. But a stream can have lots of bends and curves and so this is only a very general observation that can help in conjunction with other observations.

The tips of pines and hemlocks often point east. These trees are typically found at higher elevations and the tips are affected by prevailing winds. The operative word here is "often," not "always."

Deciduous trees, if isolated, tend to show the heaviest growth towards the south, meaning, towards the sun, usually. You might not immediately notice which side of the tree has the heaviest growth, but if you slowly walk around the tree, observing it from all sides, it should become apparent. You won't notice this in a forest since the trees are all typically growing upward, towards the light. But if the tree is solo, and you can walk all around it, you should be able to tell that there is a side that the growth is favoring. That's the south.

Back when I was in my teens, my friend Tom Kaye was a landscaper and gardener. One day he told me, "Plants have a front and a back, you know?" I thought about it, and it seemed logical, but before I had a chance to respond, Tom led me to a smallish potted tree that we could walk entirely around. "See?" said Tom, showing that the growth was sparse on the north side, and thicker and more luxuriant on the side that faced the south.

Tom wasn't interested in using trees to navigate. He just wanted the trees to grow equally on all sides, so at least in the case of his potted plants, he made a habit of regularly rotating the pots just a bit so that over the course of the year all sides would be equally exposed to the sun.

Plant Observations

Flowers often face the sun. This is where sunflowers (and the sunflower family as a whole) got their name. You can point a time-lapse camera at a sunflower and watch it move throughout the day to face the sun as the sun moves across the sky.

Many plants have long been used for general orientation. Of the many that have often been cited, I have personally observed how the leaves of prickly lettuce (*Lactuca serriola*) seem to fold up vertically, especially when it is very hot. The flat edge of the leaf faces the sun, so this is probably a water-saving mechanism by a plant that seems to survive in the poorest soil. Since the edge of the leaves often follow the sun across the sky, its other common name is "compass plant."

Keep in mind that "facing south" in these cases refers to anywhere from the south-east to the south-west, nearly a full 180 degrees of the horizon. That's certainly helpful if you're completely lost, but a compass plant is not a compass!

Goldenrods have long been used as a general direction finder, with the tips of the nodding flower heads generally facing north. There are several species of goldenrod (*Solidago spp.*) nationwide, and sometimes you will observe them mostly pointing north, and sometimes

The leaves of the prickly lettuce plant (Lactuca serriola) *sometimes point their edges to the sun. It is believed that this occurs to save moisture during hot weather. The thin edges of the leaves will sometimes point to the sun as it moves across the sky, but not always.*

not. In open fields, there is a tendency to point north, whereas in canyons where there are local prevailing winds, the flower tips will simply flow with the breeze.

Two species of genus *Silphium* have a history of being used for general orienteering. *Silphium laciniatum* (commonly known as compass plant) and *Silphium terebinthinaceum* (commonly known as rosinweed) are both members of the sunflower family with stiff leaves that stand vertically, and are said to line up with north and south. These are found mostly in the Eastern and Central US. Both were used by native people for medicine, and by pioneers for general direction-finding.

The giant saguaro cactus produces fruits in the summer on the tips of its giant "arms." These flowers, and the fruits that follow, reportedly tend to be more tightly clustered on the east side of this cactus, mostly found in Arizona, but also found in other parts of the American Southwest.

Water

Dry Ground vs. Moist Ground

Any hill or mountain range which runs in an east-west direction will retain the most moisture on the northern side. The south side will be more exposed to the sun, and will have different plant communities and will generally be drier.

Because there is less direct sun on the northern half of the range during the winter, the north side will retain snow longer, and will have more shade, and thus more ferns, moss, etc.

The practical side of this is that if you had to travel and be quiet, it would be best to walk on the northern side of the hill where there is more moisture. On the south side, there would be drier soil and dry twigs that would make more noise as you walked through.

Conversely, if you're walking along a range, it's very loud and crackly because of the dry vegetation. You might be on the southern side of an east-west range. Maybe, but not definitely. If perhaps there was a recent rain, then all that normally-dry vegetation would be quieter as you walked through it because of the moisture. If you're walking along a range and it's very quiet because of the moisture of the ferns and moist leaves, then you might be on the northern drop of an east-west range.

You'd still need to make other observations to be certain, such as observing stars, and taking recent weather patterns into account.

Rivers and Where They Flow

We've all heard it before: All rivers flow to civilization. It's been said so often that it has taken on the status of a dogmatic reality in the minds of many. If you're lost, just follow the river downstream and eventually, hopefully, you'll end up in some town. Really?

This myth has been repeated so frequently that it seems to be a fact in the minds of many, as much a "hard fact" as the moss that grows on the north sides of trees. And since it *sometimes* does work, its efficacy seems enforced. But it simply isn't always so. Just look at a map. Such "truisms" fall into the category of "old husband's tales."

If you are lost, following a stream downstream *might* lead you into a town. Sometimes. But it might also lead you into very rugged wilderness. This is not a sure-fire way to get "un-lost."

Snow Melt and Shadows

Many observations are subtle, and you look for these when there are no more obvious signs to observe.

If the terrain is snowed-in, and it's overcast, navigation can get very tricky. It can be easy to get turned around. How can you ascertain directions once you get confused?

Start to observe the snow that has piled up at the base of trees, bushes, and other plants. If you look carefully and closely, you might see a slight shadow, assuming the cloud cover is not too thick. We'll assume that the sun is in the southern part of the sky, and since it's daytime, there is light, and there can often be observed slight shadows. This would not apply if you're in a dense forest.

Also, if there has been any snowmelt at the base of trees or bushes, it will be the most obvious on the southern side of the base of the tree or bush. The back side, or north side, of the plant won't have received much sun, and there will be minimal snowmelt there.

Living Things

Birds

It has been said that the holes of woodpeckers are always on the east sides of the trees. This is demonstrably false. However, in general, the pileated woodpeckers *tend* to peck primarily on the east sides of trees. This is still a bit too imprecise to be of any practical value; plus, how

Parker examines some holes made by acorn woodpeckers in pine bark. These holes face west.

Holes from the acorn woodpeckers in pine bark. Many of the holes still contain acorns. These holes face west.

Holes made by some type of bird on the north side of eucalyptus trees.

Supposedly made by a sapsucker, these holes on a large pittosporum tree face the west.

Bird behavior might reveal some navigational clues—maybe, and maybe not.

You might learn a few things about your environment by observing the birds in the area.

many of us can differentiate between the holes made by the pileated woodpecker and any other woodpecker's holes? And suppose you actually see the woodpeckers? How many of you know the difference between the pileated woodpecker and any other woodpecker you might encounter?

I did an informal poll at an Audubon meeting to see if any of the bird-people knew how to differentiate the pileated woodpecker from any other woodpecker. To my shock, most of them actually knew the difference, and they chided me for my ignorance of birds. Okay, so it was at an Audubon meeting, and I'm not a bird person. Still, what if you just see woodpecker holes on a tree? You can't tell *which* woodpecker made the holes, just by the holes, can you?

Increasing your awareness of your natural environment is a good thing, and it isn't just about finding your direction. When you see an abundance of birds, it could be an indication that water is nearby, and that could be your lifesaver. Being lost also seems to go hand-in-hand with getting hungry and thirsty. Where there are birds circling, it possibly could mean life-saving water is nearby.

But look closely. Maybe those are vultures? Could that just mean that a dead animal is nearby?

Spider Behavior

Where I grew up, there was a hedge that faced the south. My brother and I would go stand there and observe the many spider webs that faced the south. These webs all had a little funnel shape towards the back, and if you slightly touched the web with a stick, a spider would run out and check to see if it caught a fly. All these webs faced the south, something that we never thought about because the hedge faced *only* south and there was the wall of the house behind the hedge.

In time, as we observed nature and spider webs, we noted that many spider webs nearly always face the southern direction. Nearly all—but not all—the webs we observed "faced south," but "south" was everywhere from nearly the eastern sunrise to the western sunset, nearly 180 degrees facing the southern half of space. This was not a means of precise orientation, but rather a rule of thumb for seat-of-the-pants reckoning.

Animal Tracks/Sightings

Animals are just like people. There are many sorts of "usual" behavior, and there are countless exceptions to the norm. We've all heard that animals are creatures of habit, and they will follow a regular trail from home to water to feeding just as regularly and redundantly as the human who takes the exact path to the highway to work to the store and home again, day after day. Usually. There are enough exceptions to normal animal behavior that in some way relates to your ability to navigate that you must consider all such observations as general guidelines and general rules-of-thumb, but nowhere as neat and tidy as the direction of the compass needle.

Animal trails and runs can be found all throughout North America. Could these help you navigate your way through the forest or desert, from your Point A to your Point B? Maybe, maybe not.

After you've spent some time outdoors observing signs of animals, it's likely that you'll notice animal tracks and trails *everywhere.* And animals are creatures of habit, even more than you are. They travel from the spot they sleep to find food and water every day. Each animal has its own "territory" and its own "home range," and these are not the same. The territory of, for example, a bear, would be akin to your own house and yard. In the case of the bear, each bear considers its territory its own. The home range is akin to your daily travels to the store, workplace, library, post office, etc. The bears' territories generally do not overlap, unless their population gets too big for a given area. And the home range can extend for miles and extends way beyond their own territory.

Bears and smaller animals leave their marks in the grass and depressions in the soil, wherever they go. Sometimes these trails are subtle and hard to spot, and other times they are very obvious.

But does spotting and following these trails help you if you are lost? Remember, the animal isn't coming into town to visit the grocery store and post office. Still, as survival instructor Ron Hood often pointed out to me, following an animal's trail might lead you to water. Might. Following the animal trail might also lead you to a good hidden spot for a shelter, but it might not. So although there is value in being able to observe animals' trails, there's really no guarantee that following them will get you where *you* are trying to get to. Observing animal trails can be a useful tool, and it's a tool more useful for your nature awareness and overall orientation.

Clouds

Can you determine *something* about navigation from the observation of clouds? The short answer is "no." The more detailed answer is "maybe."

First, you should get a primer on meteorology, something easy to digest like Eric Sloane's *Weather Book*, where the author shows you the general patterns of weather systems. You begin by learning

Clouds are fascinating to watch, and generally they reveal only marginal information which helps with navigation.

about some of the most basic types of clouds, and what they mean for short-term weather forecasting. And then, you should learn how weather systems operate, how the low pressure systems that bring storms and rain typically (but not always) move counter-clockwise, rotating slowly (or quickly) as they travel eastward across North America. High pressure weather systems rotate clockwise, and thus the clouds rotate clockwise, still all moving eastward across North America.

Watching the direction in which clouds move can give you a very limited sense of direction, and your ability to do this depends largely upon your having other bits of data to compare to. Cloud-watching is another clue to your current environment, but it's not likely to be an important tool in your natural navigating.

If you want to get better at natural navigation, don't become fixated on just one thing. The observation that you have always relied upon in your home territory may not be there in your new location. Observe all things.

The First Time I Got Lost

During the summers when I was in high school, I stayed on my grandfather's farm in eastern Ohio. It was a fifty-one-acre farm, with an old farmhouse, and a huge old barn. There was an orchard in the front, a small hill, and a huge field where crops were planted. Along the north side were orchards and wild plants. And in the back—the west side—there was a dense forest, with a small stream that flowed through it.

When I arrived for my first summer, my uncle took me out back, through the field and through the woods, past a dirt road which defined the western border of the farm, and out to a lake that a neighbor had made. The neighbor was a lawyer who lived in Cleveland, and only came out here occasionally. My uncle said it was okay to come out to the lake during the hot days of summer and swim.

A few days later, when my uncle was away at work, I decided to go out again to check out the lake, and study some of the plants of the area. I headed out through the large field, and entered the woods where I remembered my uncle entered. There was no discernable trail, so I just tried to follow where my uncle had walked. The woods were full of branches and brambles, and I was forced to walk this way and that. It was so dense that you could not see the sunlight in the forest.

So I just kept walking towards the lake, avoiding the thorns of the berry vines, moving out of the way of the poison oak, and stopping here and there to look at unusual plants that I'd never seen before. Eventually, I came to a clearing, but the road wasn't there. Instead, the forest opened to a grassy field. I assumed that I'd wandered a bit to the south, so I just kept walking straight, figuring I'd come to the road, and then the road would lead me to the lake. I was already tired and deep in sweat from the heat of the day and the humidity of the forest.

I kept walking over a slight hill and wondered why I saw no road. Before long, there was a farm house, which I assumed had to be the home of the farmer who lived out back down the road somewhere.

As I approached the old farm house, I observed all the things stored by the house, and the large barn off to the left, the buckets and hoses and other farm implements. Suddenly I stopped and looked around and I was dumbstruck! That was our farm house I was looking at! How was it possible that I was 180 degrees off course?

It was a very unusual moment of realizing how easy it was to get lost!

I turned around and was determined to get to the lake. I walked back to the woods and found the slight opening that my uncle had shown me. I entered.

This time, I didn't just casually walk through the woods. I deliberately lined up two trees and walked in a straight line, as much as was possible through the thick woods. I lined up two more trees, and took a beeline again, straight towards the far end of the woods where I believed the lake to be. This time, I was observant of the barely-noticeable trail through the woods that others had taken. There was the semblance of path, though it was not obvious. I kept lining up two trees so I would walk in a straight line, and I continued very deliberately that way. Before long, I found the road, and just down the road a bit, there was the lake!

I went swimming, and then easily found my way back through the woods to the farm house. After a summer of going through the woods, I never got lost again, because eventually I knew each tree and turn in the trail. I knew the forest.

I learned to be extra observant the first time in new territory, to avoid that very uncomfortable feeling of being lost.

If you're like me, the feeling of being lost is very uncomfortable and you never want that to happen. There is probably no such thing as the so-called "natural" sense of direction – that is something you develop with practice, experience, and familiarity with a given territory.

QUIZ:

1. Woodpeckers always make holes on the east side of trees. True or False?
2. Moss always grows on the north sides of trees. True or False?
3. Spiders generally build their nests facing south because their brains have a function which tells them where North is located. True or False?

ANSWERS

1. False.
2. False.
3. False. They face south because it's warmer there.

ACTION:

Take a walk through your neighborhood or a local wild area where there are trees. Look for animals' markings on the trees. Look at how the trees might lean. Observe whether the tree is thicker on one side or another. After you've made several observations, determine if any of these could have assisted you if you'd been lost.

CHAPTER TWO

THE SUN

A lot can be learned by simply observing the path of the sun throughout the year. All ancient civilizations studied the sun, and were well aware of the sun's apparent path as it traveled through the sky, and how this path changed from the winter solstice to the summer solstice. A lot of this we take for granted because we have been taught some of the basics of how our earth (and solar system) operate from childhood. But ancient man did not have the advantage of textbooks or model globes that spun on their axis; they learned by direct observation, and then they passed on this information through oral tradition, written records, and even in the orientation of key buildings and monuments.

Many of the observations of the sun relate to the concept and reckoning of "time." The passage of the sun through the sky can be readily measured by a shadow, and thus a linear distance can be equated with a set passage of time (as with the sundial).

BASIC OBSERVATION

If you want to record the sun's changing path, you can do so in any area where you have a clear view of the horizon. On December 21, the winter solstice, the sun rises at the southern-most point of the eastern horizon. Drive two vertical stakes into the ground, whereby you can site the rising sun over the top of both stakes. In the days and weeks that follow, you can site over those two stakes and observe that the sun is no longer rising in that same spot. As the days get longer from December 21, the sun rises a bit more to the north, day by day. By the time June 21 comes around—the summer solstice—you will notice that the sun is now rising significantly north of where it rose on the winter solstice. If you want to record that northern-most rising of the sun, drive a third stake into the ground whereby when you site over stake one and stake three, you are looking right at the rising sun of the longest day of the year.

But let's say you don't have your modern calendar. Simply by sighting the sunrise each morning from a given point, starting from sometime in summer, you can watch how the sun rises farther and farther south on the eastern horizon. Then one day, the rising sun doesn't seem to move any further south. It appears to rise in the same spot for three or four days. You just discovered the winter solstice. And then, as you continue to observe the rising sun, day by day, it begins its slow movement back to the north. Each day it rises just slightly farther north. And then, in about six full moons of observation, the sun rises in the most extreme northern edge of its journey. It rises in the same spot for three or four days. You just discovered the summer solstice. Then, day by day, the sun rises a bit farther south along the eastern horizon.

We know that this very basic observation was of utmost importance to ancient cultures, because standing stones, monuments, cairns, pyramids, churches, and many other methods have been devised to measure the movement of the sun worldwide. People have long built permanent means to measure the solstices and equinoxes, as well as the cycle of the moon and planets.

The purpose of knowing the annual cycles of the sun and moon range from mundane to esoteric. The mundane include such tasks as basic reckoning of directions (the point of this book), and the telling of time (during the day, or throughout the year), as well as knowing when to plant and harvest crops. The esoteric includes knowing the precise days to have important ceremonies to coincide with the internal cycles of each human body, or to correspond with the important days of the "gods" (however that is defined by each culture).

ECLIPTIC

The ecliptic is the apparent path of the sun across the canopy of the sky, from east to west. The path isn't parallel to the equator, however. The ecliptic is not the celestial equator—the celestial equator is an imaginary plane which extends out into space from the actual equator. The ecliptic, however, is the band of the sky through which the sun, moon, and planets appear to travel, and this band is tilted in relation to the celestial equator at an angle of 23½ degrees. Yes, it sounds crazy and confusing the first time you hear this, but look at the illustration and this will start to make sense.

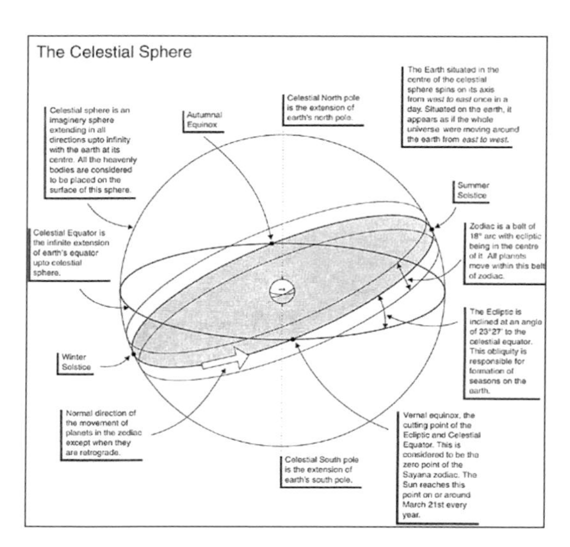

A view illustrating how the ecliptic—the path of the sun and moon—is offset from the celestial equator at an angle of 23½ degrees.

The sun and the moon travel within this imaginary 16 to 18 degree wide band (depending on what astronomer you're reading), called the zodiac—the middle of which is called the ecliptic, and this band rotates across the sky at a 23½ degree angle from the celestial equator. Once you learn to recognize this zone, you'll start to recognize several familiar constellations.

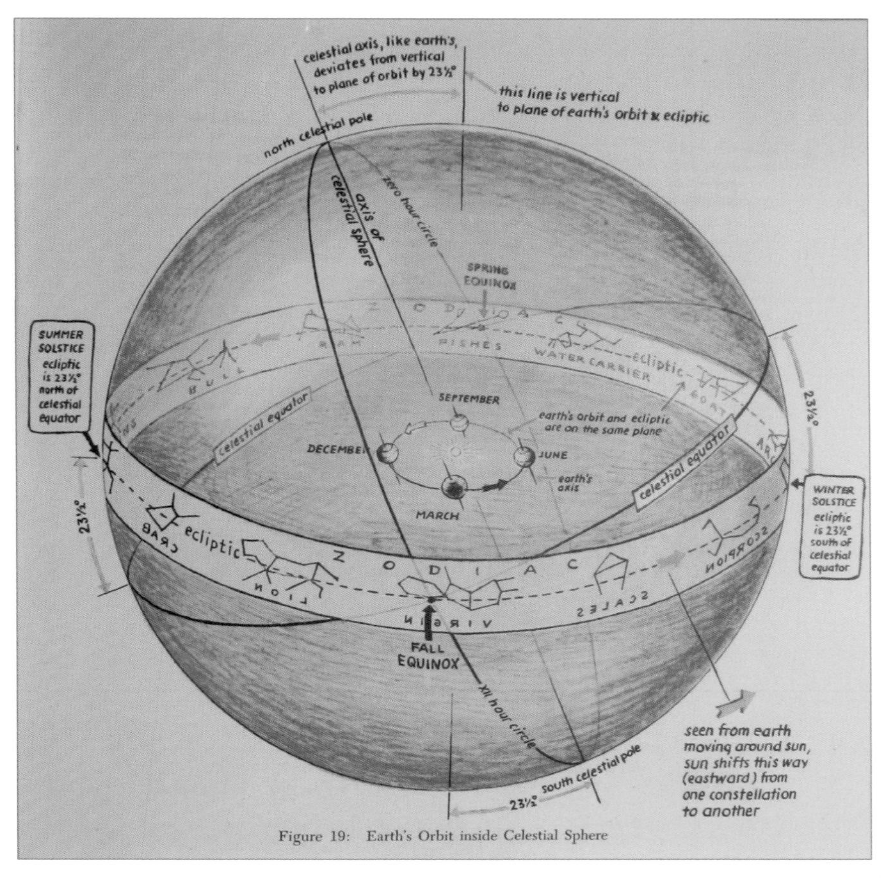

Figure 19: Earth's Orbit inside Celestial Sphere

Showing the Earth's orbit inside the Celestial Sphere. This is the best depiction I've seen that clearly shows the nature of the ecliptic, from the vantage point of earth, through the year. Here is the original caption from H.A. Rey's **The Stars,** ***in the chapter on "Ecliptic and Seasons": As on all our models, proportions on this one are not drawn to scale. Sun is too small, earth too big, and sky globe much too small in relation to orbit. Pole Star on sky globe's top ought to be many miles away, so that earth's orbit, including sun, shrinks to a pinpoint in comparison with globe. The four separate axes piercing the tiny earth globe on our model would melt into one, and practically coincide with the celestial axis, as is the case in nature. Such inaccuracies are unavoidable but, once explained, become irrelevant.***

[Drawing from *THE STARS: A New Way to See Them*, by H.A. Rey. Copyright 1952, 1962, 1967, 1970, 1975, 1976 by H.A. Rey. Reprinted by permission of Houghton Mifflin Harcourt Publishing Company.

The Sun is a major indicator of direction.

The sun rises in the east, slowly moves across the sky, and sets into the west. That's the general idea, though it's a bit more complex than that.

For very basic navigation, you can follow the path of the sun in a technique known as "hand-railing." This means that you keep a prominent terrain or celestial feature to one side of your body—left or right—to help keep you on a course. For example, by moving along the imaginary line that the sun travels throughout the day, and keeping the sun to your left, you will be able to fairly easily walk in a consistently westerly direction. Or in the reverse case, if you need to walk in a consistently easterly direction, you keep the sun to your right as you walk along.

Seasonal changes in the sun's pattern

One of the most basic "seat-of-the-pants" methods of determining directions by the sun is to observe the sun. Right? This works fairly well on a daily basis. But because of the steady seasonal changes in the sun's relation to the earth, the sun does not always rise in the same spot on the eastern horizon, and doesn't always set in the same spot on the western horizon.

As they say in the aviation industry, "Reaching your target is a constant series of minor corrections."

TIME AND THE SUN

What we call "time" is actually a very local thing. When people used sundials, they were measuring Local Apparent Solar Time, which is the local time. This meant that every town and community kept their own time, making coordinating time over great distances problematical.

By 1884, as a result of a long process, an international congress in Washington established what we now call Standard Time. Standard Time means that the entire earth was divided into twenty-four vertical zones, each about 15 degrees of longitude wide.

This means that anywhere inside a given time zone when we call it 5 a.m., the sun can rise an hour earlier on the eastern side of the time zone than the western end.

Time as currently calculated is a modern abstraction! It helps us with the ability to coordinate complicated lives.

Note: Keep in Mind that a Twenty-Four-Hour Day and "Time Zones" are an Abstraction.

To re-state, the earth is divided into twenty-four sections, each 15 degrees wide. Twenty-four times zones of 15 degrees each, and 24 times 15 equals 360. In our modern convention, the circle is divided into 360 degrees.

Hmmm, where did that come from? Why don't we divide the circle into a more even number, like 100? The simplest answer is that it came from the ancient Sumerians, and we've followed it ever since. Such numbers may not seem organic, or related to anything on earth, but with a bit of digging, you can understand the logic of this system.

Making a simple sun compass/sun clock

OBSERVING A SHADOW

This is a good way to begin observing the path of the sun, especially if you've relied upon clocks and compasses your whole life.

You can create a mechanism which serves as both the sundial and sun compass. It will work best within local areas, and the margin of error will increase the further you travel. Okay, let's try it.

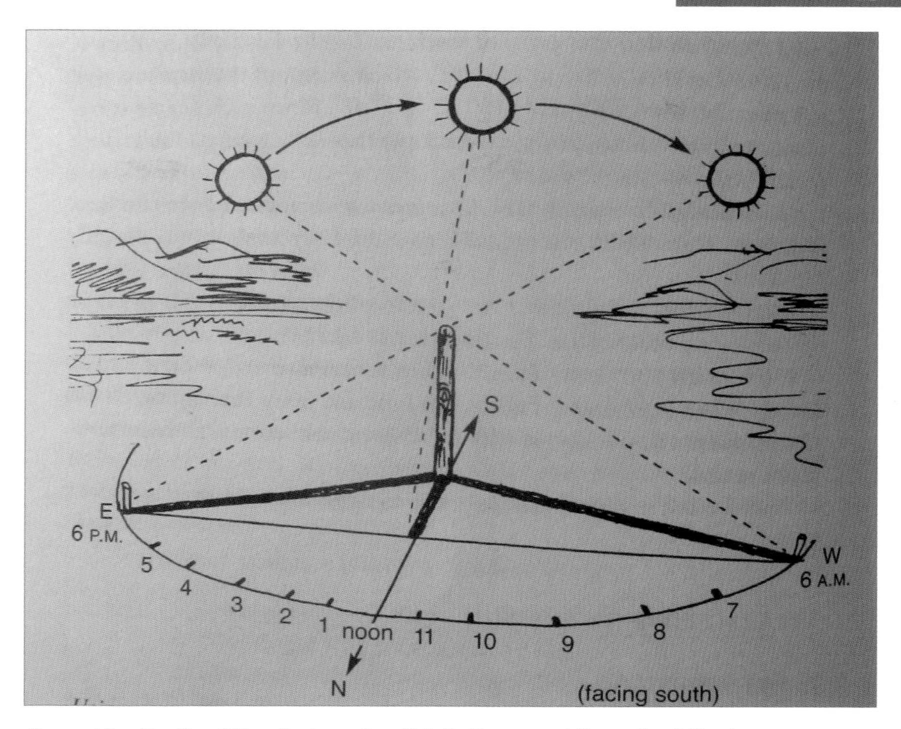

By marking the tip of the shadow of a stick in the ground throughout the day, you can create both a crude compass and a crude clock.

An upright stick is placed in the ground. The tip of its shadow is marked with a pebble.

As the shadow from the stick moves, mark the tip of the new shadow with another pebble.

Every few minutes, continue to mark the tip of the stick's shadow with another pebble.

After you've marked the tip of the shadow several times, you will note a line forming. This will be an east-west line. The shortest line to the shadow stick will define a north-south line.

Pound a stick into the ground. Make sure it's solid, and not wobbly. Now put a pebble at the end of the shadow. Wait twenty minutes or so. The shadow will have moved, so put another pebble at the end of the shadow. Wait another twenty minutes and do this again.

In general, when you are in the northern hemisphere, your shadow will be pointing generally northward if the stick is stuck vertically into the ground.

The shadow's movement, marked by the pebbles, will be eastward, because the sun moves westward. The shadow should be the shortest around noon, when the sun is directly overhead (directly overhead at 1 p.m. if there is Daylight Saving Time).

If you now draw a straight line from the stick to the stone marking the shortest shadow, you should have a north-south line, more or less. A perpendicular line gives you an east-west line, and your crude compass.

This is most accurate around the summer solstice, when the days are of equal length, and it's also most accurate if created around mid-day.

If you know the approximate time that the sun is rising and setting, you can evenly divide the arc formed by the stones and create a crude, but usable, sundial clock.

If you are camping out with Scouts or friends, make this stick sun dial large so everyone can see it easily and refer to it during the day. Locate it in the most open area, where it will receive sunlight throughout the entire day, with no interference from the shadows of trees.

You have just made your first crude solar compass, as well as a primitive clock. And it all seemed so simple and easy—and it was! Still, if you want more accuracy with your compasses and clocks, you'll need greater complexity.

"It is important to hold on to the idea that there is nothing about the movement of the sun that cannot be understood by putting a stick in the ground and watching its shadow."
—Tristan Gooley

A Sundial Is a Much More Precise Instrument than a Stick in the Ground.

Making a sundial allows you to utilize all of the principles that pertain to the observed movements of the sun across the sky, and the various methods that have been devised to create a standard for time. After you've made your first sundial, you'll have joined the ranks of amateur astronomers.

Many years ago, I read an article in the May/June issue of *Mother Earth News* by Carmen Trisler, who makes tiny sundials inside aspirin tins. The idea was that you could make it small, carry it around in your pocket, and then just set it up somewhere when you wanted to know the time.

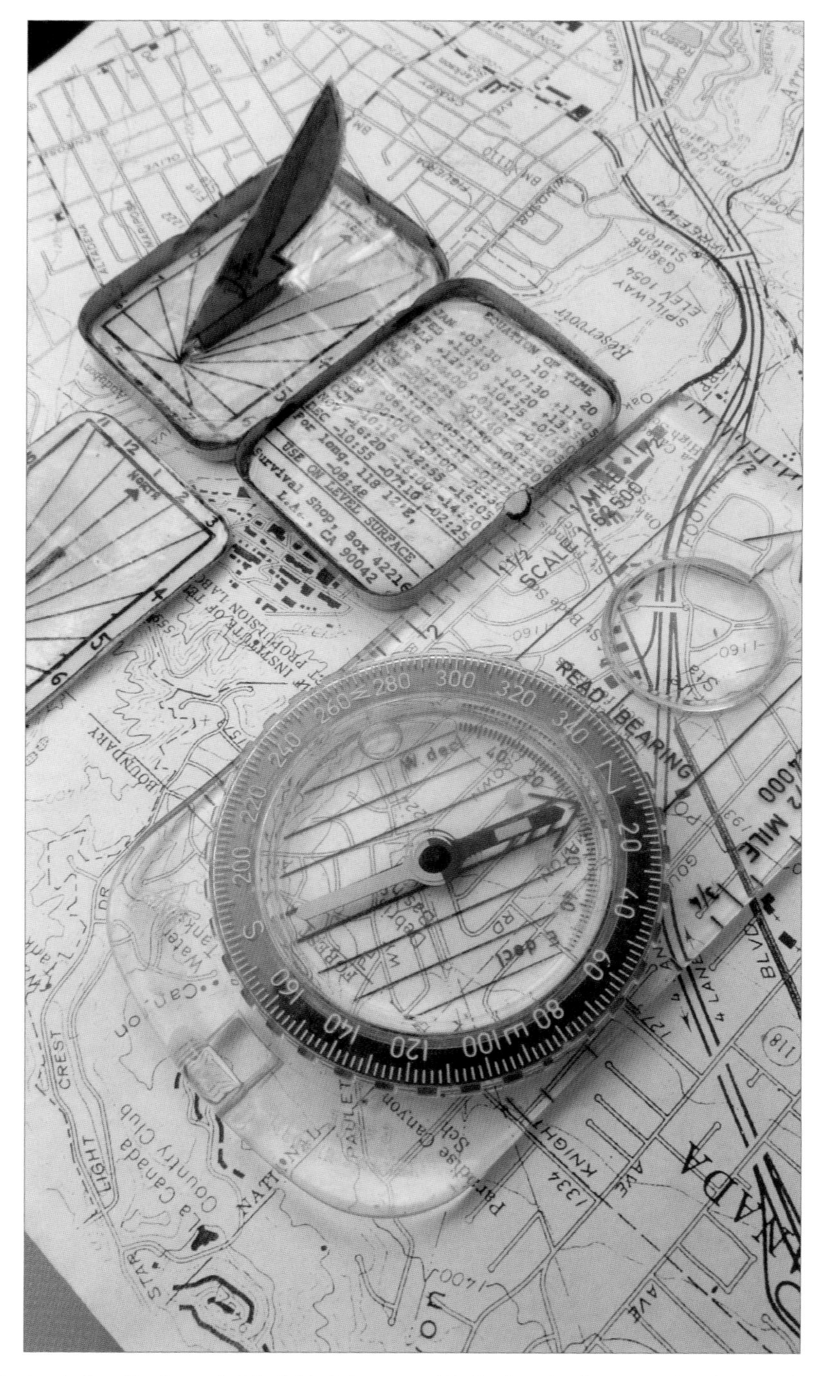

A simple localized sundial that fits into an aspirin tin is actually accurate when made well and adjusted for location.

But since I rarely buy aspirin, it didn't make sense to buy the container of aspirin just for the tin, so I saved the article for years in one of my many files.

Then one day it happened! A worker who was doing some carpentry at our home discarded an empty aspirin tin in my trash can. I picked it out as soon as I spotted it, knowing I could now proceed with this long-awaited project.

With the tin in hand, I quickly shuttled through my files of clippings, trying to find the old article. Amazingly, even with my eclectic system of filing, I found it! The article described how to make a useful sundial which folds into the aspirin tin. All I had to do, the article proclaimed, was to cut out (or copy) the clock face from the magazine, mount it onto cardboard, and then put it into the tin. A simple one-size-fits-all sundial!

I made a photocopy of the clock face, as well as the gnomon (pointer), secured them both to cardboard, and cut them out. That done, all I had to do next, according to the magazine article, was to attach the gnomon to the clock face, set the sundial on a flat surface in a sunny location, and align it to True North with my compass.

All this done, I was now supposed to be able to simply read the time by observing where the top of the gnomon's shadow appeared on the clock face. Wrong!

The time on my clock face was nearly an hour wrong. (I had already taken Daylight Saving Time into consideration.)

I then carefully re-read the old article, and noted that its author stated the sundial would provide "approximate time." But I wasn't satisfied with approximate time. After all, I can guess within an hour of actual time by merely glancing at the position of the sun.

I then began my serious research into the intricacies of accurate sundials.

Making a sundial indeed requires knowledge of the compass and an understanding of the directions and divisions of time. But because it is essentially about time-keeping, and not about direction-finding (which is the point of this book), you can learn how to make your own sundial in one of the references listed in the rear of this book.

THE SETTING SUN

Quick Ways to Determine How Much Time (Usable Light) you have before Sunset

This is an old way to tell approximately how long it will be until the sun sets. When I was first taught this system from Abbie Keith of the Sierra Madre Search and Rescue team, he said this was a Navajo method. When, many years later, Ron Hood talked about the same method, he said it was Shoshone. Of course, probably everyone who lived close to the land figured this out.

Face the horizon and extend your arm. Tuck in your thumb. Bend your hand so that your fingers are parallel to the horizon. Now, using your four fingers, measure up from the horizon to the sun. Each finger represents about fifteen minutes of the sun's travel across the sky. If you are standing somewhere where you cannot actually see the western

As described in the text, you can measure how many hours until the sun hits the horizon by measuring the width of your hand, with each hand's distance equating to roughly one hour of the sun's travel in the sky. Here, Dorothy Wong extends her right hand, with thumb tucked in, so that the bottom of her hand is on the horizon.

Dorothy now brings her left hand on top of her right hand.

Dorothy brings her right hand on top of her left hand, and continues this way until she gets to the sun. Each "hand" equals about one hour of the sun's travel.

horizon, you should just assume that the horizon is where your eyes look when you are standing erect and looking out perpendicular from your body.

Though everyone's finger size and length of arm is different, this still works pretty well for most people. When I actually knew the time that the sun would set by having consulted sunset tables, I was able

Facing the horizon, begin by putting the bottom of one hand at the horizon.

The left hand now is placed over the right hand.

to calculate with my fingers to within four minutes of the actual legal standard time.

This will give you a good idea when the sun hits the horizon. Keep in mind that in the summer, there will still be usable light for at least an hour after sundown. In the winter, things will get pretty dark very soon after the sun dips below the horizon.

Continue to leap-frog one hand over the other until you reach the sun. Each "hand" distance equals one hour of the sun's travel.

If you need to make camp before dark, this is a good way to determine how much light is left.

The Moment of Sunset

You've probably read in your newspaper the time of sunset for a particular day. But since the earth is curved, the exact moment of sunset will vary depending on your longitude. So the time you read in the newspaper is just standard over a wide area, and everyone within a time zone will experience the exact moment of sunset at different moments.

I have long read in outdoor literature—mostly the books by Bradford Angier—that if you watch the sunset until it actually dips below the horizon, you will see a green flash. The famous green flash! I have looked many times, but never noticed this, and so I put it into the category of old husband's tales, right along with all rivers lead to civilization, and moss grows on the north sides of trees, and the lost Dutchman mine, and secret fishing holes where the big one got away.

One day I was out in the Big Tujunga wash in the hilly area of Northern Los Angeles County, collecting herbs, and I had an unobstructed view of the western horizon. The sky was clear, without clouds. The sun was low and touching the horizon. So I took a seat on a large rock to watch the show. As the sun sank lower and lower, I observed around and about the sun, not exactly looking right at it. As the sun nearly made its way below the horizon, I noticed the optical illusion of the remaining speck of sun flattening out, seeming to be twice as wide as it actually is. Then the sun disappeared as I watched, and I saw the green flash. It was not a green flash on the horizon, but a green flash in my field of vision, an optical illusion of green that lasted for a second or so. Then it was over.

I've observed this at least once more under similar circumstances.

Though this has very limited practical use for orientation or telling time, it's still an interesting natural phenomenon that you've likely heard about.

Learn to Observe Shadows and How to Use Them to Navigate.

How to use sunlight even during cloudy/overcast weather when it's not as obvious or easy to see: Take a stick and place it vertically into the ground, or even just stand the stick vertically on your hand. Carefully observe the base for any hint of a shadow. Lift the stick up, and then back down again. Did you observe the slight shadow? Try moving your body to face another direction, and try again. Move the stick up and down, slowly. Do you see a shadow? Usually, you will detect a very slight shadow as you move the stick. This can help you in a general way for determining your orientation.

Using your Analog Watch to Determine Directions

This is an old technique that still has some relevance.

Your analog watch can double as a compass, assuming it is keeping accurate time. Hold your watch flat and point the hour hand at the sun. The halfway point between the hour hand and 12 will point south. If it's Daylight Saving Time, you should use the halfway point between the hour hand and 1 to point south.

What if the sun is obscured by clouds? Hold a match or twig vertically along the edge of the watch, and turn the watch until the match's faint shadow falls directly on the hour hand. The hour hand is now pointing at the sun, and you can determine south.

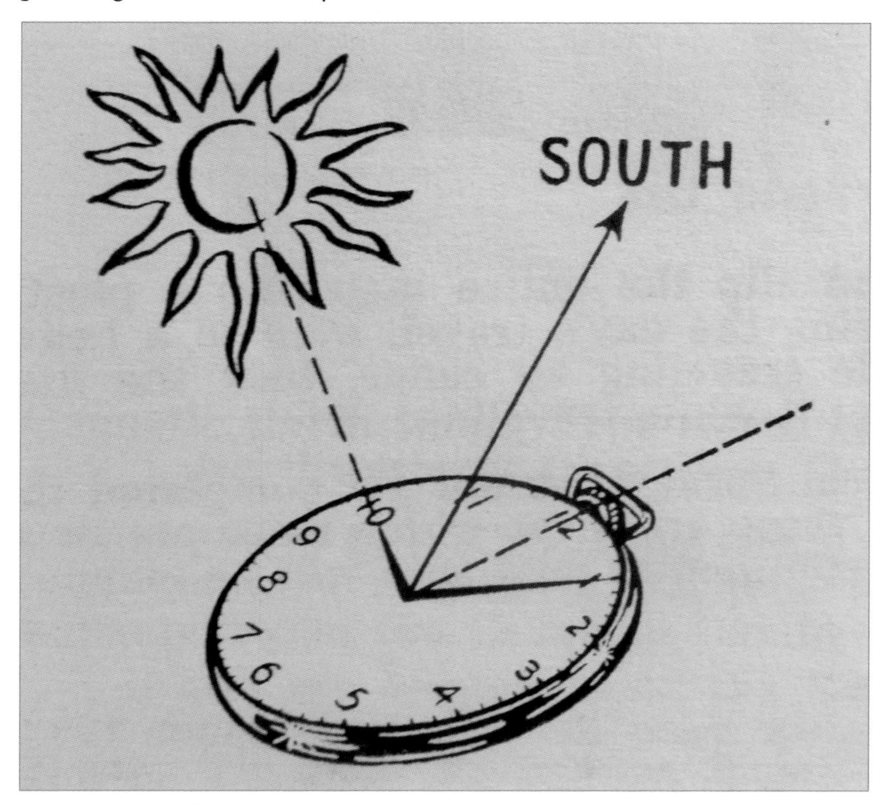

Point the hour hand of your analog watch towards the sun. Halfway between that hour and 12 is south. This works in the Northern Hemisphere.

Unless it's extremely overcast, you should be able to see at least a faint shadow.

Whoa! Don't most people have digital watches these days? Right. So here's a little trick that might seem silly, but should work.

Your digital watch says it's 3 o'clock. Draw a round clock face on a piece of paper, and write in at least the 3 and the 12 on your clock face. Hold that paper flat, and point the 3 at the sun. Yes, this works just as well with a clock face that you draw on a piece of paper, again, assuming your digital watch is keeping correct time.

Keep in mind that the change in angle with the sun's arc with latitude can result in inaccuracies with this watch method. This works best at certain latitudes, and it works best at midday. Like every other makeshift observation, you want to take other observations into account as well.

QUIZ:

1. Everywhere within a given time zone, the sun will appear to rise at exactly the same time. True or False?
2. "Ecliptic" is what happens to the moon or sun during an eclipse. True or False?

ANSWER

1. False. If you're observing from the west end of a particular time zone, the sun will rise an hour later than from the east end of that time zone.
2. False. The ecliptic is that band of sky where we observe the travel of the sun and moon. It's also known as the band of the zodiac.

Action

In a flat sunny area, drive a vertical stick into the ground. Put a little pebble at the tip of its shadow. Wait awhile. As the sun moves across the sky, the shadow will move. Put another pebble at the tip of the shadow. Do this a few times, and note the path of the tip of the shadows—the path defined by the pebbles you placed there. Think of this as your mini-Stonehenge, and your understanding of the perceived path of the sun.

CHAPTER THREE

THE NIGHT SKY: THE STARS AND THE MOON

Understanding the Night Sky: Basic Principles

To gain a basic understanding of the movement of the stars, an introductory course in astronomy would be very valuable. Here is a very basic explanation of the stars and their apparent movement.

First, go outside on a clear night and observe whatever stars you can see. You may or may not know the constellations, so just observe what you see and attempt to take note of various patterns or shapes. Then, take a break. Go back inside, have a coffee, and then go back outside in an hour and look again at the stars. Hey! Those stars are not in the same location as an hour ago! What happened? Initially, you will think, well, the stars all moved, and yes, from your earth perspective, they did "move."

However, what you observed was the fact that the earth revolved. The earth is constantly moving, rotating around and around, just like the model earth that every classroom has.

Now that you have observed that the stars appear to move, make some more specific observations. You don't yet know any constellations, and you aren't even sure what the term "constellation" means.

But when you go outside, find a spot that you can go back to, where you can sight the stars in relation to some fixed point. The top of the neighbor's house will do. Go look at everything you see. Just observe. You'll notice slightly different colors of stars—which are actually distant suns, like the one our earth revolves around. Look for patterns, such as groups of stars that seem to make up a triangle, or a square, or lines. Keep in mind that these stars are probably hundreds of light-years apart, all traveling in some different direction. They just *seem* to be somehow related as you view the sky as if it were a two-dimensional flat space.

Now, come back in an hour, and look at those same stars. Yes, they moved! Well, the earth moved. Note in what direction they moved, since knowing how the stars appear to rotate in the sky can be helpful in determining general directions.

Now, let's start by getting to know the North Star.

Getting to Know the North Star (Polaris)

Q: The North Star is the brightest star in the sky. True or False? Ask this to an average group of people, and you will get a majority saying yes. But the answer is False.

The North Star is not the brightest star in the sky. However, it is highly significant for finding directions.

If you follow it with time-lapse photography, the North Star will appear to be stationary, and all the other stars will appear to rotate counterclockwise around it. If you were standing on the North Pole, the North Star would be directly overhead. Time lapse photography is capturing the rotation of the earth. So if you've ever seen a photo where all the stars appear to rotate around a single point, that single point is the North Star!

So, first, let's find the North Star. Begin by locating the Big Dipper. The North Star is in a direct line with the two end stars of the Big Dipper (see illustration). If you're just starting out, you should determine where the northern part of the sky is located, so you're not looking in the wrong part of the sky. If you don't already know where north is in your area, get a map of your area; all standard maps have north located at the top.

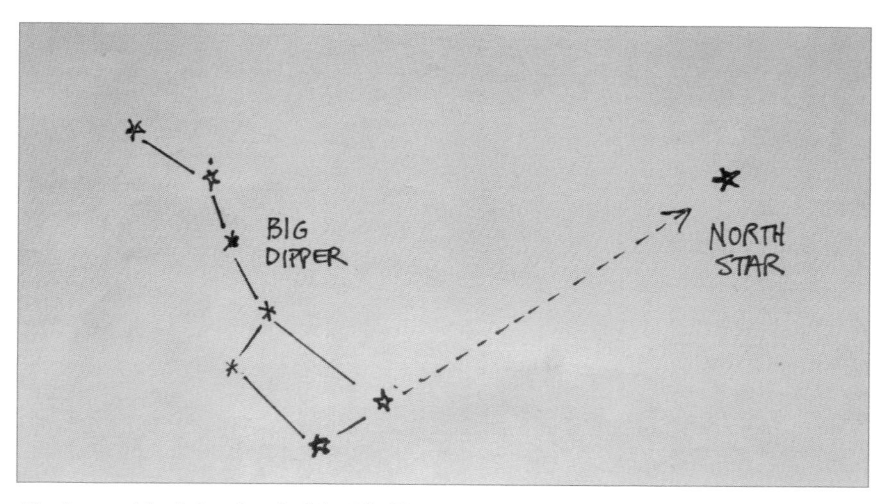

The two end "pointer stars" of the Big Dipper point directly towards the North Star.

Go outside on a clear night to your viewing spot and face the north. If you live in a rural area, there may be so many visible stars that it could be hard to make out distinct constellations. You might even see the Milky Way. If you live near or in an urban area, you're only going to see the brightest stars because the light from the city obscures the less bright stars.

Are you able to discern the Big Dipper? In this combination of stars, ancient people saw a large water dipper, as if it were scooping water.

Locate the outer two stars that comprise the "dipper." We call that distance X. Those two stars are in a direct line to the North Star. If you continue a line with a distance of 5X in the direction that the dipper would be pouring, you find the North Star!

Now that you've located the North Star and the Big Dipper, take a note of its location. Come back in an hour. *Whoa*! What happened? The earth rotated, and though the North Star appears to be in pretty much the same location, the Big Dipper has now rotated counterclockwise by 15 degrees in the sky. Come back in another hour, and the Big Dipper will have rotated another 15 degrees in the sky, counterclockwise. You're witnessing the great clock face of the sky, with the North Star smack in the middle.

Now you know how to find north at night, assuming it's a cloudless night. (Also, we're assuming that you're north of the equator. At the equator, you won't see the North Star at all, because it will be right on the horizon. And if you live in the southern hemisphere—well, let's just say that the rest of this chapter won't have much relevance to you.)

SIMPLEST CALCULATION

If you can find north, you obviously can find south, and perpendicular to your imaginary north-south line is east and west. If you can find the North Star in the Northern Hemisphere, you now know all your cardinal points!

THE SIDEREAL DAY

In a twenty-four-hour period, the Big Dipper and all the stars will appear to rotate around the North Star. Well, almost twenty-four hours. In fact, if you're standing at your fixed sighting point, and you observe the Big Dipper at a fixed location at 9 p.m., you'll see it again at that fixed location in twenty-three hours and fifty-six minutes, a time known as the sidereal day, which is four minutes shorter than the solar day. This sidereal day is the amount of time it takes for the stars to get back to a fixed location. This means that at 9 p.m. at your fixed point of observation, you will observe the Big Dipper in a particular spot, but three months later at 9 p.m., those four minutes will have added up so that the Big Dipper will be in a very different spot. From our primary perspective of using the stars to determine the cardinal directions, this isn't an issue; this only becomes an issue when you begin to use the stars to determine accurate time.

Note: What we call the Big Dipper is just a part of the larger constellation known as the Great Bear, or Ursa Major. The handle of the dipper is the tail of the great bear. Ursa Major is probably the most widely known constellation. There are countless stories and myths about it.

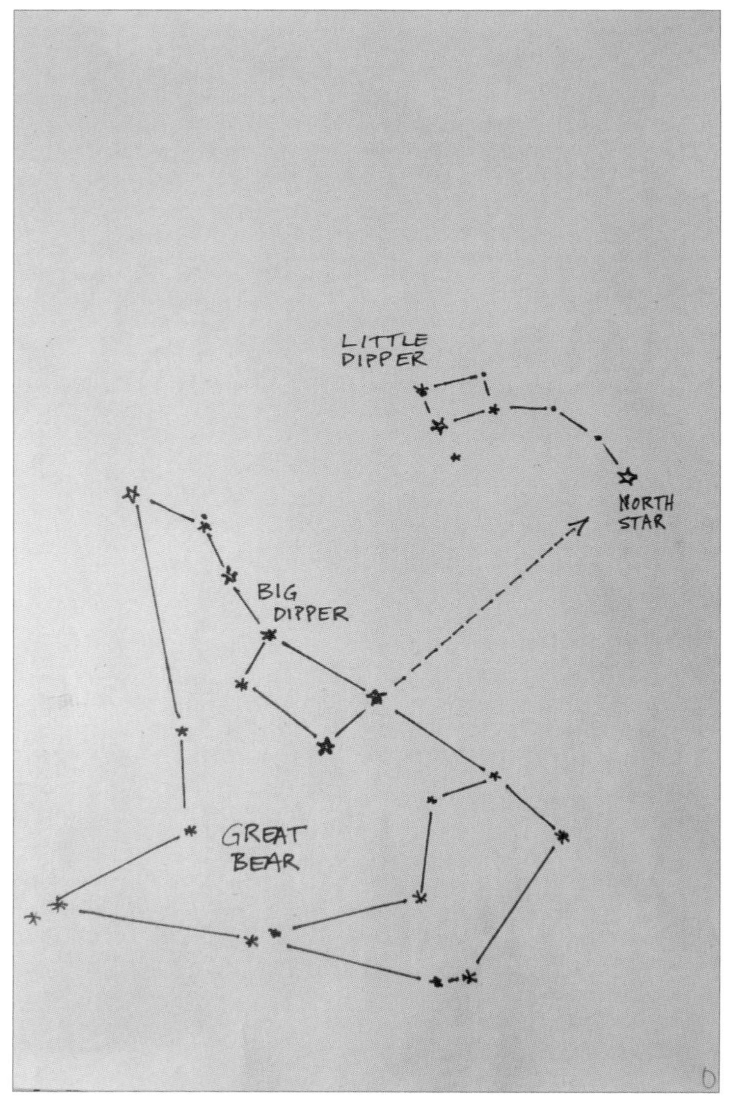

The Big Dipper is part of the Great Bear (Ursa Major) constellation.

Now, because you're viewing the North Star from a particular location in the northern hemisphere, it will always appear in the sky as high above the horizon as your latitude. That means, for example, since I live at 34 degrees above the equator, I can measure 34 degrees above the horizon with a protractor in order to try and locate the North Star.

How do I know I live 34 degrees above the equator? I read it on a map! But if I didn't know that, I could use a protractor to see how high the North Star is above the horizon where I live, and that angle equals my latitude.

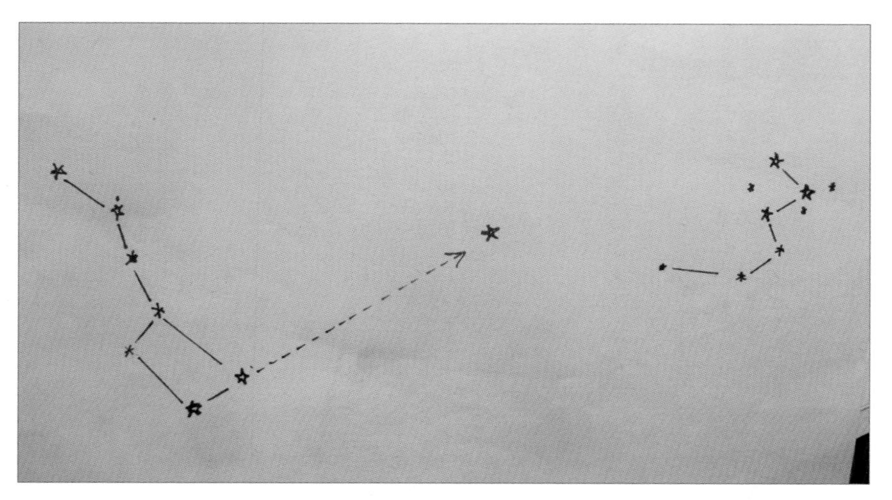

The Big Dipper and Cassiopeia appear to rotate counterclockwise around the North Star (in the Northern Hemisphere).

As the Big Dipper rotates counterclockwise around the North Star, it will sometimes be below your visible horizon. Now it's time to get familiar with another grouping of stars called Cassiopeia.

GETTING TO KNOW CASSIOPEIA

Cassiopeia is located on the opposite side of the North Star from the Big Dipper. Cassiopeia means The Queen, and ancient people saw a seated lady in their imaginations when they looked at this cluster of stars. When I first saw Cassiopeia one night, when the Big Dipper was below the horizon, I thought, *That sorta looks like the Big Dipper, but it's like a sloppy Big Dipper with a few stars missing.* Some people call this constellation the big M or big W, which more accurately describes the shape of the brightest stars of the constellation.

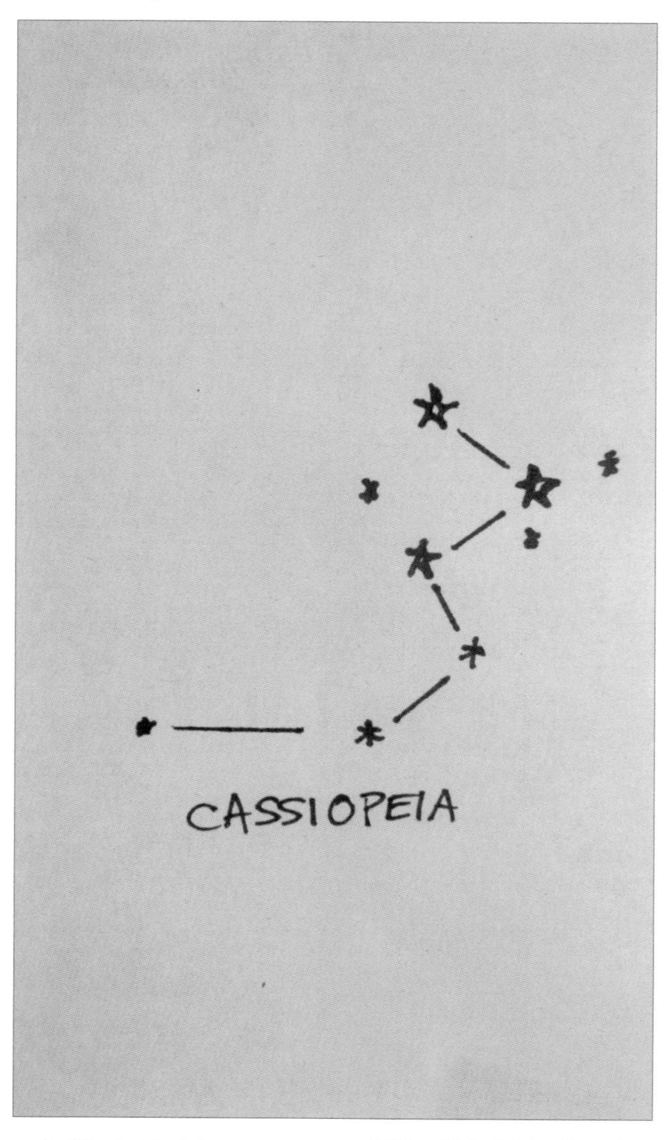

Cassiopeia—the "Seated Lady"—appears as an "M" or "W" of stars. It rotates counter-clockwise around the North Star, on the opposite side of the North Star from the Big Dipper.

If you spot Cassiopeia, you can spot the North Star. Cassiopeia is found roughly the same distance away from the North Star as the Big Dipper, and roughly speaking, at the opposite side of the North Star. So, Cassiopeia rotates counterclockwise around the North Star at roughly 180 degrees from the Big Dipper. This mean you can use Cassiopeia in the same manner as the Big Dipper to locate the North Star.

To reiterate, once you've found the North Star, you know the whole terrain. Turn your back to the North Star and you are facing south, and to your right is the west, and to your left is the east.

A SEMI-CLOUDY NIGHT

You're now aware that all stars appear to rotate counterclockwise around the North Star. But the night is a bit cloudy, with just a few stars here and there visible. How can you determine directions?

From a fixed location, begin to observe the stars you can see. This could be a bit challenging, because the clouds will continue to move. Still, if you can see certain stars, watch them to see the direction in which they are moving.

If the stars appear to be rising, you are facing east. If the stars appear to be dropping in the sky, you're facing west. If you can mentally visualize all the stars, slowly rotating counterclockwise around the North Star, this makes perfect sense.

If you're looking in the southern sky, the stars will appear to be moving flatly to your right. Looking to the north can be a little challenging. If you're sighting above the North Star, the stars will appear to be moving flatly to your left. However, if the patch of stars you're viewing lie under the North Star, their movement will be a somewhat flat swing to your right.

As long as you grasp the fact that all the stars appear to rotate counterclockwise around the North Star, you'll be able to look at the movement of stars over the course of an hour or so and determine your cardinal directions. It's not particularly complex, but it works, and it might really help if you're "confused."

CONSTELLATION

What is a constellation anyway?

We touched upon this briefly, but let's try to explain it more fully.

Hundreds of years ago, star observers would note specific configurations of stars that might look like a square, or an animal, or a triangle, or some other object. They would take note of that grouping of stars, and after a while, these groupings of stars were given a name, like the Big Bear.

But each of the stars that we see in one of these constellations are not related to each other in any way. They just *seem* to have some relationship, because of their relative closeness, from our earth vantage point. In fact, in any groupings of stars in a given section of space, the stars could be hundreds—even thousands—of lightyears apart from each other.

People have seen groupings of stars that look like things for thousands of years. Most of the names that we call these groupings have come down to us over time. We've already talked about a few of these—the Big Dipper (actually a part of Ursa Major constellation), and Cassiopeia.

Ancient constellations were named for whatever figure people saw in the sky, like Leo the lion, or Orion the hunter.

By 1930, astronomers worldwide decided to bring some order to our view of the sky, and so they defined boundaries of eighty-eight constellations, and gave them Latin names. Today, sky watchers and astronomers all use this accepted system. Any time you read about star-gazing and how to identify the constellations, this standard system is followed.

WHAT IS THE ZODIAC?

Though you don't have to be a professional astronomer to enjoy the sky, it does help to know some of the terminology used to describe the sky and the activities we see up there.

For example, we all hear the word "zodiac," and somehow we're pretty certain that it has something to do with astrology and horoscopes.

From our observation on earth, the path that the sun and moon follow in the sky, as well as the path of the principal planets, is known as the ecliptic. This imaginary band in the sky is 15 degrees high, and astronomers have divided it into divisions, each 30 degrees wide. The center of this band is called the ecliptic by astronomers, which we talked about in Chapter One.

It is in this path that ancient people have noted and charted constellations. Each of these divisions of the sky—30 degrees wide—is named for a constellation, which are mostly named for animals. Zodiac means "circle of animals."

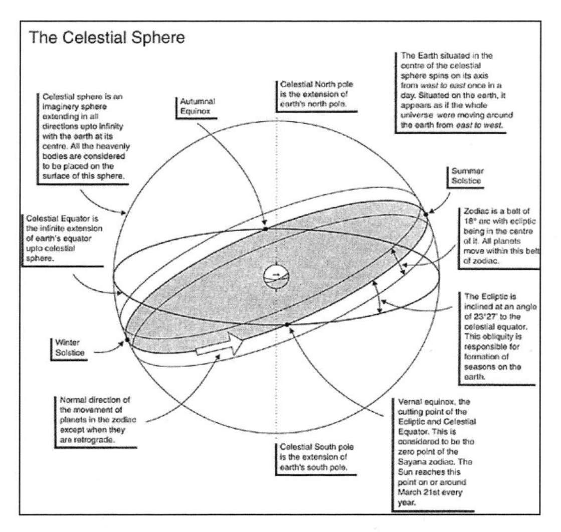

This illustration explains a lot about the heavens which we observe from earth, and why the stars move the way they do.

Remember, if you extend an imaginary plane out into space from the earth's equator, you have the celestial equator. The path of the ecliptic—the zodiacal belt—moves across the celestial equator at an angle of 23.5 degrees. That might sound complicated, but just look at the illustration.

We know that ancient people were aware of this angle of the ecliptic, because this knowledge appears to have been built into the mathematics of many ancient monuments in North and South America, in Ireland and Western Europe, in India, in the stone circles of Southern Africa, and many other places.

Once you get to know the observed path of the sun, and the observed path of the moon, in the area where you live, you'll have grasped a greater understanding of the night sky. One of the best ways to grasp the way the stars seem to move is to simply go to a local observatory where they occasionally show videos depicting the changes of the stars throughout the seasons. Or just go in your backyard and sit and watch for long enough to see the stars changing.

Keep in mind that, with the exception of the moon and planets and the occasional comet, all the stars appear to move and rotate together, as if they were all on one plane. This is an illusion, of course, but in the course of your lifetime, all the visible stars are going to appear to create the same shapes in the sky. Visible changes in what we see in the night sky takes hundreds of years, if not longer.

GETTING TO KNOW ORION

Orion is an easy to recognize constellation, probably the most widely-known constellation after the Big Dipper.

Orion is said to resemble a hunter, with a shield, and a raised club. Four conspicuous stars provide a general outline for his body, and three stars in a line define his belt. From his belt hangs his sword. Below him is his dog, in the Big Dog constellation (*Canis major*) with the brightest star in the sky, Sirius, or the dog star, being the brightest in the sky.

Orion is easily noted, and the constellation travels across the sky just to the south of the ecliptic. This means that, roughly speaking, Orion rises in the east and sets in the west, just like the sun or moon.

If you're lost and you can see Orion, you might be able to re-orient yourself.

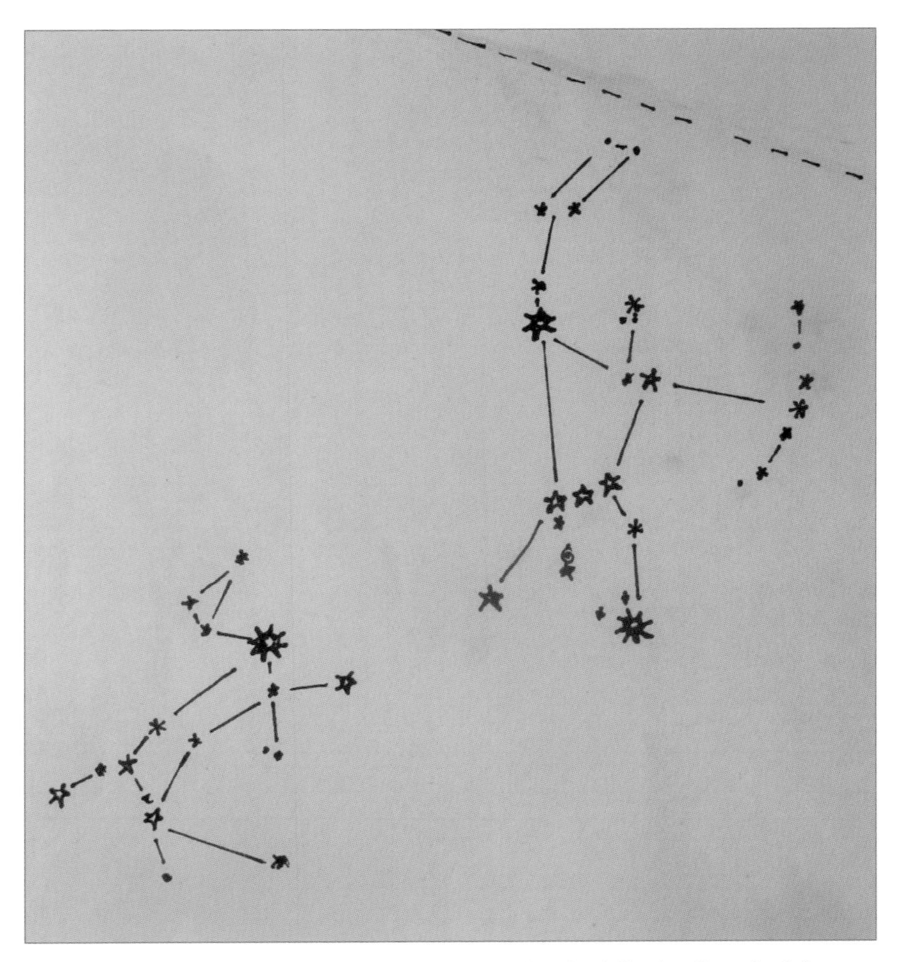

The distinctive constellation of Orion moves across the sky, following the celestial equator. This makes Orion ideally suited for night navigation.

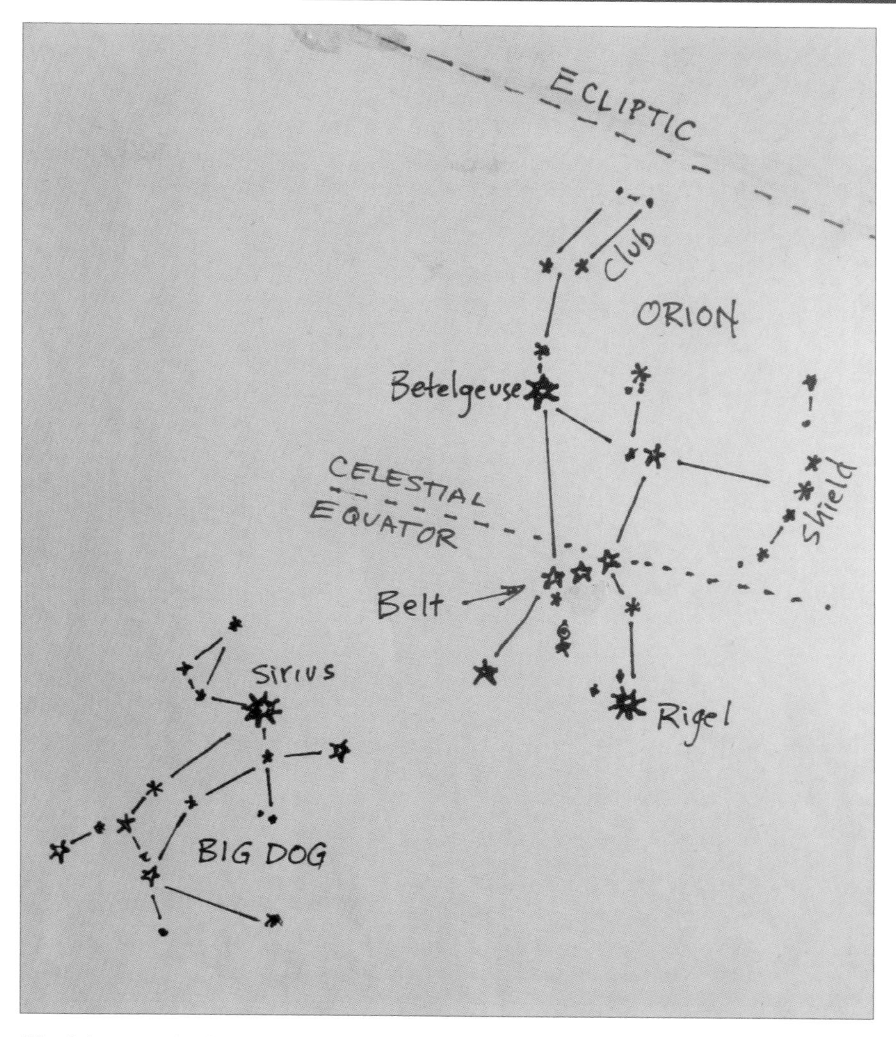

The Orion complex labeled.

A TRUE URBAN MYTH

Once while driving in an unfamiliar part of Los Angeles with a friend, my friend and I got hopelessly lost. We were east of East LA, somewhere, and we didn't recognize the names of the streets and all the stores were unfamiliar. After we drove around in circles, I was able to just stick my head out the window until I could see some stars. I could barely believe it, but I saw the Big Dipper, and so now I knew where was north, and thus where everything else was. We turned around, headed north, and soon everything looked familiar again. We made it to our destination, and didn't have to spend the night lost in LA.

THE MOON

Moon Shadow

Remember how we put a stick in the ground on a sunny day and then put a pebble at the end of its shadow? We did that to create a solar compass to determine a north-south line. [See illustration on page 29 to refresh yourself on those details.]

Guess what? You can do the same thing with the shadow of the moon. Put a stick in the ground in an open area where it's exposed to the moon. Put a pebble at the tip of the shadow, and every 15 minutes or so, add another pebble to the shadow tip. Then, you draw a line connecting the shadow-tips, and that forms an east-west line. The shortest line from this line to the stick is the north-south line.

Obviously, this works best during a full moon, but can be done at any phase of the moon that casts a sufficient shadow.

BLUE MOON

The term "once in a blue moon" has today come to mean the second full moon that occurs in a given month. However, the term *originally* referred to the occurrence of four moons in a season. Normally, in either spring, summer, winter, or fall, there are three moons. When there are four moons in a season, the third of those four was *originally* referred to as the "blue moon." The details of the reasoning can be found in the *1937 Maine Farmers' Almanac.* Also, this original definition of a "blue moon" occurs more rarely than the second-full-moon-in-a-month definition.

QUIZ:

1. "Zodiac" means "circle of animals." True or False?
2. The North Star is the brightest star in the sky. True or False?
3. In the northern hemisphere, when you look up to the night sky, all the stars appear to rotate clockwise around the North Star. True or False?

ANSWERS

1. True
2. False. The North Star, aka Polaris, is actually only the forty-eighth brightest star in the sky.
3. False. All the stars appear to rotate counter-clockwise around the North Star.

ACTION

Go stand outside and find the North Star and observe the stars around it. Ideally, try to locate the Big Dipper or Cassiopeia. Note where these other stars are located in relation to the North Star. Look again in approximately an hour. Note how the North Star appears in the same spot, but how the other stars have moved. Observe how much the stars have moved in an hour. Check again in another hour.

CHAPTER FOUR

THE MAP

"Understand your map, and you'll understand your world."

S. I. Hayakawa spent considerable time in his classic *Language in Thought and Action* demonstrating that you should not confuse the map for the territory. In his case, the verbal description that we make of the actual world is just that—the description. And the description is not the real world. Hayakawa drives home the point that only by refining your linguistic abilities will your description bear a close resemblance to the real world.

A map is the description. The territory that your map describes is the real world all around you. A lot of effort has gone into making modern maps more and more accurate, especially topographical maps. Take the time to understand your map and it will speak forth to you as a 3D impression of the terrain you hope to travel.

THE MAP

You need to get from Point A to Point Z on foot. You've never done that before, so you'll have some challenges. To help overcome those challenges, you should get a map of your territory and a compass. But let's say you only have the map.

A map of your terrain is always more important than the compass, though you should always consider them as a unit.

The map is an aerial picture of your terrain, showing you the location of roads, buildings, water, towns, railroad lines, mines—everything you need to know. A topographical map is the map of choice because it gives you a visual depiction of the rise and fall of the land. This enables you to choose the easiest route (which is not necessarily the shortest) between two points.

Yes, there are countless sorts of maps made for various reasons.

ROAD MAPS

A road map from the auto club is great if you're traveling from Los Angeles to Cleveland, but it's not of much value if you get off the main highways. Because this is a special purpose map, it doesn't even need to be to scale because you're traveling on a freeway or highway, and you're just following the numbers, and watching for the posted highway signs as you travel.

GEOLOGICAL MAPS

There are maps that depict earthquake faults, and the dominant types of minerals found in a given area. These are great for geologists, geology students, and miners.

HIKING MAPS

Hiking is very popular and there are maps that primarily show the hiking trails in great detail. If you plan to hike the Pacific Crest Trail, for example, you can get a whole book of maps that tells you not only where to camp for the nights, but where to get water, where the stores and lodging are located, and possible places to cache some goods in some of the long stretches.

FLIGHT PATHS

Maps that are used by pilots tell them the flight paths to follow, and it lets the pilot know where to expect other aircrafts. These are important tools for all pilots, and it helps to keep our air space organized and trouble-free. While these can be very interesting to the non-pilot, they are really not useful unless you're flying.

LOCAL SPECIAL INTEREST MAPS

These can be any map privately made for the layout of a farm, a state park, a large zoo, a large campsite, Disneyland, etc. Occasionally, these maps will be designed and laid out so they fit into a little booklet that can be given to visitors.

In one case, I was trying to find a lake that was listed in the northeast corner of a large botanical garden. I could not find it, until I realized that they printed their map with south at the top. I automatically assumed that north is at the top of all maps, but there are exceptions. In this case, when I finally noticed the little star they printed on the map showing where north should be, I was able to rotate the map in the proper alignment and I found the lake right away.

TOPOGRAPHICAL MAPS

For our purposes, we're going to focus upon topographical maps, the map of a specific portion of the terrain, drawn in such a way that it should tell you everything you need to know about the terrain you're walking in, things like rivers and springs, rises and falls in elevation, remote buildings, railroad lines, aqueducts, and, of course, roads, freeways, and all the urban infrastructure.

First, you need to purchase a topographical map for your territory. Make certain that you're buying the most current map of your area.

WHERE TO BUY?

Map stores

Some local map stores offer a complete offering of the US Geological Survey's topographical maps for all areas. Map stores usually offer other maps as well, such as locally-made maps, 3-D maps, and others.

Online

You can buy any official US government map from the US Geological Survey, and these can be purchased online. Go to www.USGS.com. Though you can print some out on your home computer, I much prefer the pre-printed maps to the full dimension of the topographical map.

USING A TOPOGRAPHICAL MAP

Okay, you have your map. Let's take a tour. Lay it flat on a large table. Pretend you're in an airplane, and you're looking down on your terrain. The topographical map is very much like looking down at a photo, except that everything is encoded and color-coded.

- Brown are the contour lines, which represent the rise and fall of the elevation.
- Blue signifies a water feature.
- Green is vegetation.
- Black lines represent manmade features, such as water towers, buildings, power lines, roads, and trails.
- Red typically indicates major highways.
- Magenta/purple are revisions made to the map from previous versions.

In addition to the different colors, many objects can share the same color but mean different things. For instance, dashed blue lines signify a seasonal stream. A solid blue line means water that typically runs year-round. A single row of black dashed lines means a manmade trail, while two parallel dashed lines means a dirt road wide enough for a vehicle. It is important one understands the meaning of all map symbols so you can accurately translate the symbols as you look at the map into what the actual terrain will look like.

Learn to identify major terrain features:

- Peaks
- Ridges
- Spurs
- Draws
- Saddles
- Depressions

Also understand just because a map shows certain water features, they might not always be there! If the map shows a stream, it is very likely a seasonal stream that you won't find in the summer when you need it. In many cases, the same holds true for springs.

Begin by just observing all the lines, marks, symbols, and colors of the map. Since it's a map of your area, you should be able to identify a lot of things on the map right away, such as the lake to your north, or the railroad line that meanders to the east of town, or the freeway just to the south of your home.

If you're unclear about what any of the symbols on your map means, we've reprinted some of the common ones here to refer to.

A topographical map shows you the contour of the land—the changes of elevation—that you do not see on a typical road or trail map. The contour of the landscape is depicted by brown lines that represent the rise or fall of the elevation. You'll see these lines more or less parallel, and each map will indicate the elevation gain between lines. At the bottom of the map, you'll read something like "contour interval 40 feet." The actual distance between lines is determined by the flatness or steepness of the landscape. Where the lines are far apart,

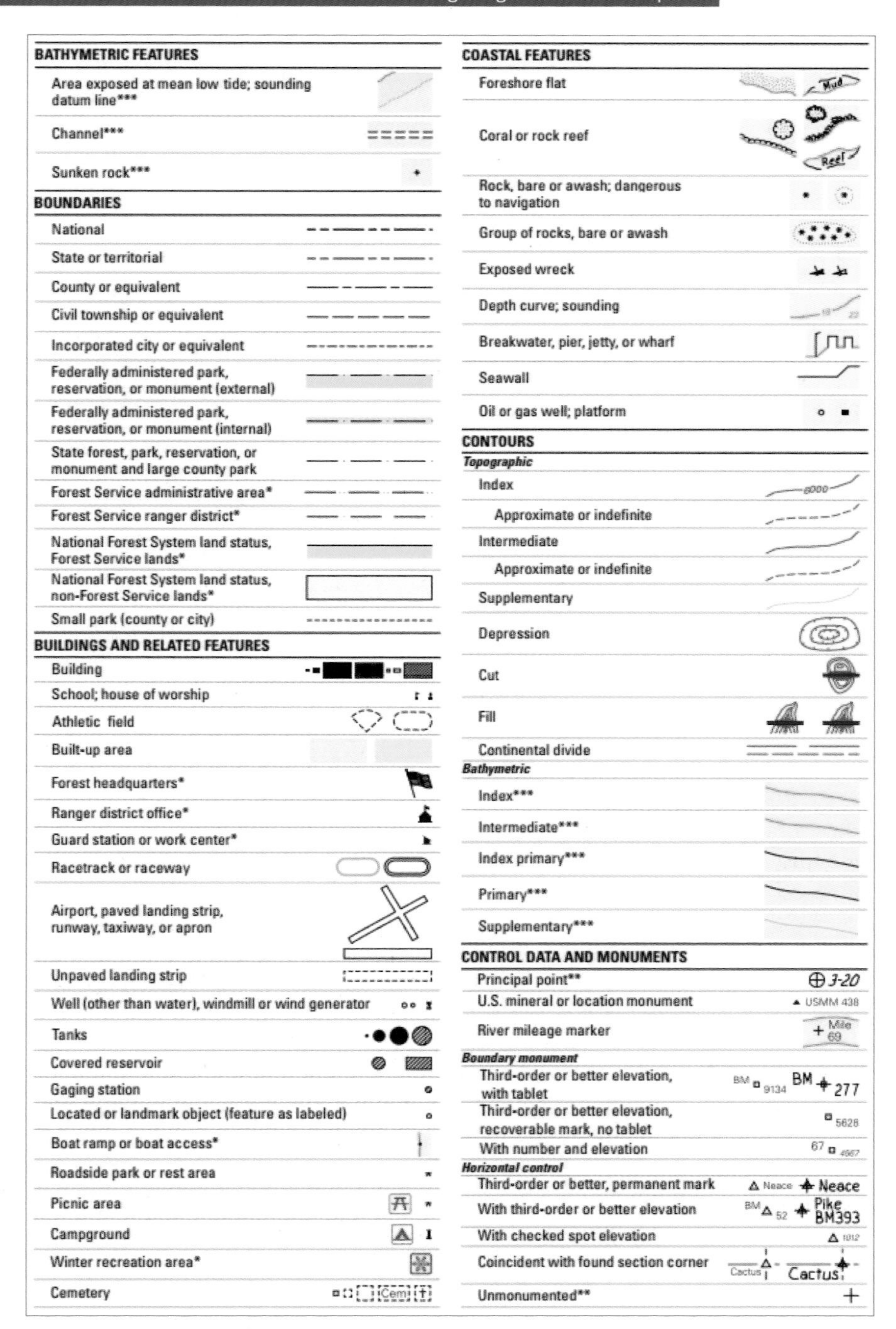

Common symbols used on topographical maps.

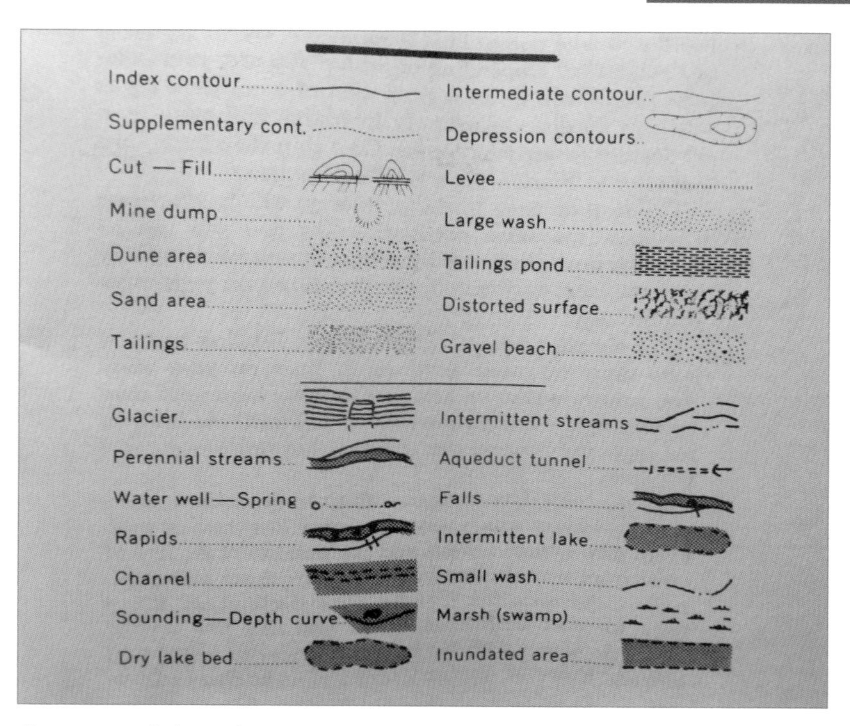

Common symbols used on topographical maps.

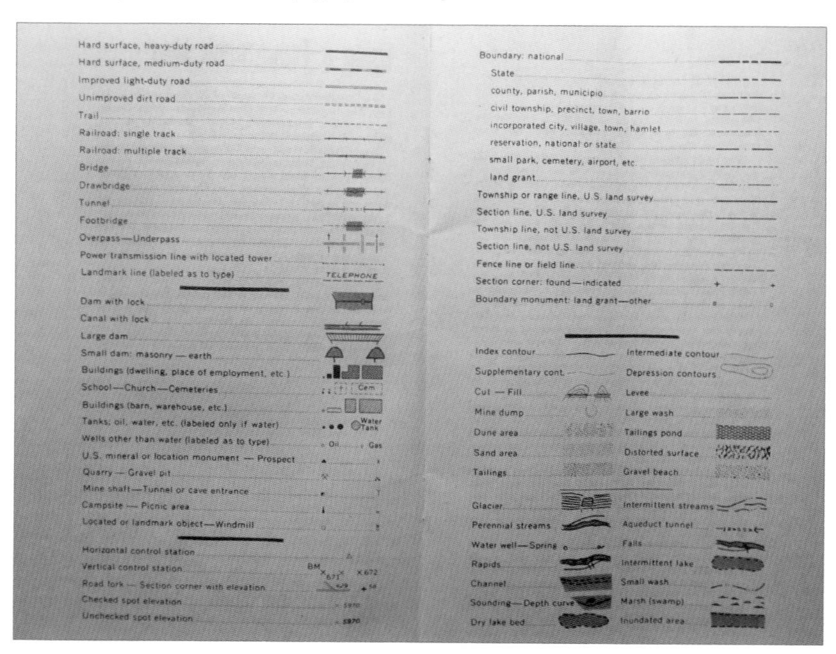

Common symbols used on topographical maps.

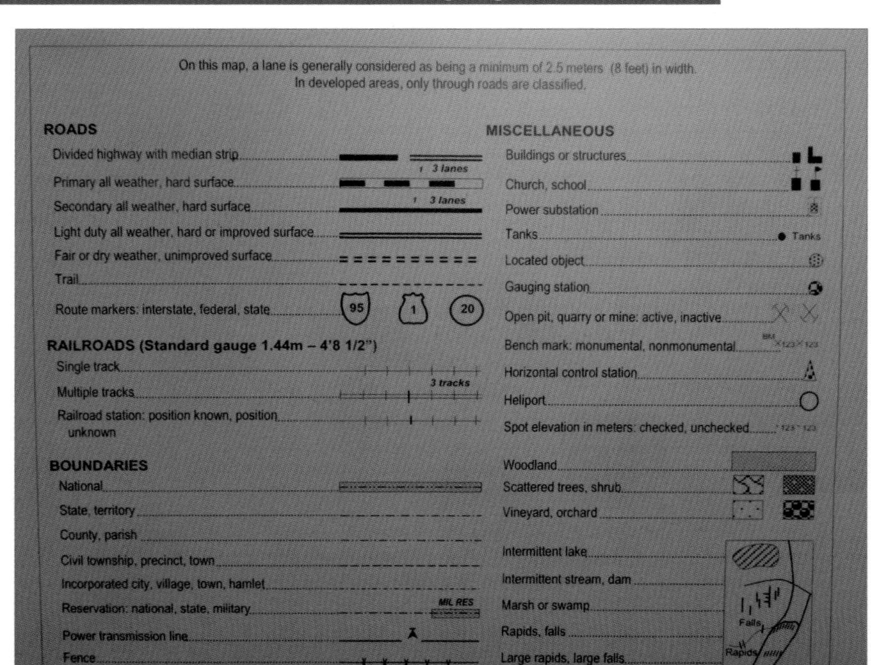

Common symbols used on topographical maps.

the territory is nearly flat, like desert land. Where you see lines all tight together, you should be visualizing steep hillsides.

Study the map until you can visualize the rise and fall of the terrain. Note that the rivers are the low points in the terrain, and the hills typically rise from the river bottom. If you're viewing the very top of a hill, it might be designated by a topographic line that is in the shape of an oval or circle. The topographic map also includes the actual elevation above sea level at measured points, so you can look at the map and determine the elevation at any given point.

One of the many practical applications of understanding these topographical lines comes when planning a route of travel. If you only want to travel in a straight line, that's easy to chart, but it might be difficult to travel, if the straight line goes up and over a hill. If you want the *easiest* route from your point to your destination, then you should chart a course that allows you to *stay within the map's topographic lines* as much as possible. That is, if you chart a course that stays within the

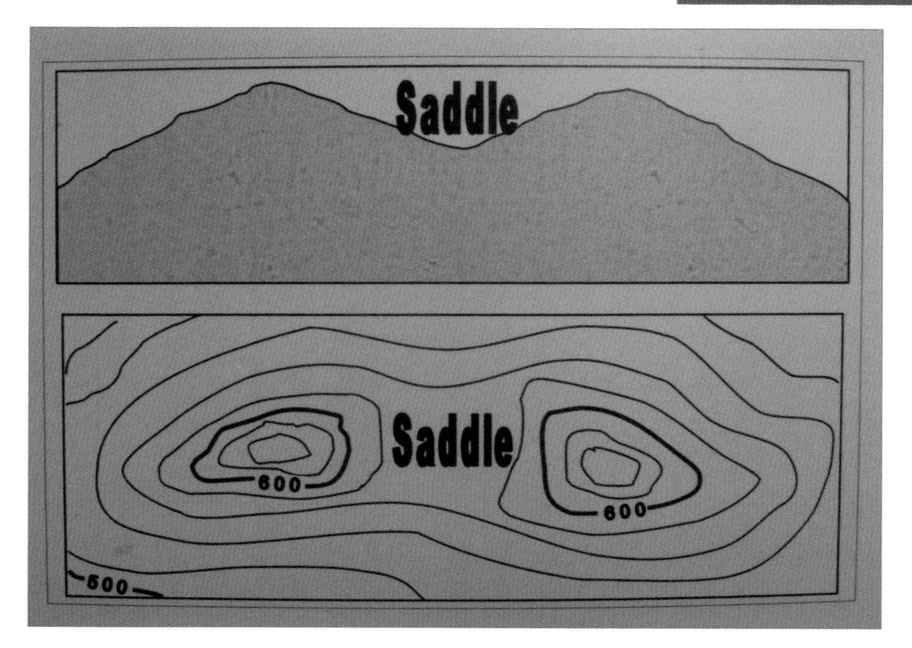

The topographical lines are designed to illustrate the 3-D world on flat paper. See how it's done?

topographic lines, your path will only have minimal elevation gain or loss. That means you're working less, and working smarter.

Conversely, if your charted course is constantly crossing topographical lines, you've chose a path that is all uphill, or downhill, or both.

SCALE OF THE MAP

The three most commonly-used scales for the topographical maps are 1 unit to 250,000 units; 1 to 62,500 units; and 1 to 24,000 units.

The bigger number means that more territory is covered on the map.

1:250,000 map

This scale means that one inch on the map represents 250,000 inches in the field, or pretty close to one map inch represents four miles of territory. A map like this covers a lot of territory, and gives you the broadest view of your terrain within a distance of about one hundred miles.

1:62,500 map

This scale of one map inch to 62,500 inches in the field translates to about each map inch corresponding to about a mile in the field.

1:24,000 map (7.5 minute map)

With this scale, one map inch equals 2,000 feet, which is a common surveying distance. These maps cover from forty-nine to sixty-eight square miles, and are one of the most commonly-used maps, because they give enough detail within a reasonable area.

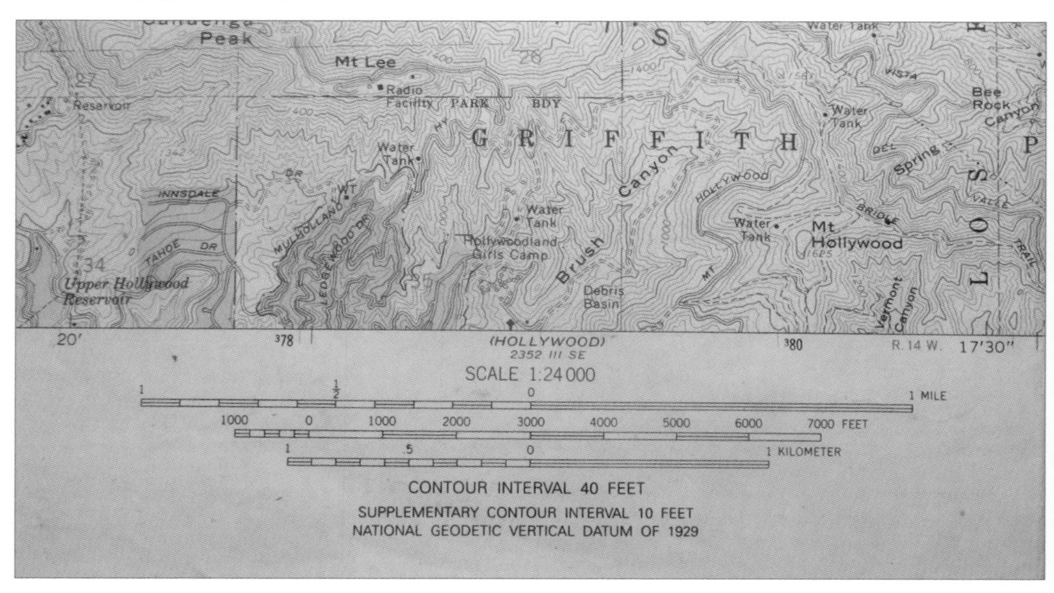

The scale of a map is typically given at the bottom, such as this map with an indicated scale of 1:24,000.

The smaller the scale, the more detail there is, though less area is covered. Think of this as zooming in to an area with your camera. The more you zoom into a spot, the more detail will come into focus, but the tradeoff is that less area fills the frame.

ALIGNING YOUR MAP WITH THE TERRAIN, WITHOUT A COMPASS

The first step to accurately using your map is to align it with the terrain. Remember, you don't have a compass yet, but there are still a few ways to do this.

Remember, True North (grid north) is always at the top of your topographical map. To get started, lay your map out on a table.

ALIGNMENT WITH THE SUN

You've learned in chapter one how to create a simple low-tech compass with the sun, by placing sticks in the ground. Do this now and determine north. This is not entirely accurate and your "north" may be off by a few or many degrees. Still, this will get you started.

Once you've determined north with your stick shadow, go ahead and turn your map so that the top of the map aligns with the north, as best as you've figured so far.

VISUAL ALIGNMENT

A visual alignment of your map with the terrain is probably the best way to navigate. This requires you to be in an area that is high enough, or clear enough, so you see many obvious landmarks in at least three directions, and preferably more.

Lay your map down flat, preferably on a table. Look at that water tower to your southwest, and turn your map so that a pencil line drawn between where you think you are to the water tower will continue in a straight line to that actual water tower. Then look up to the north at a tall peak with some sort of radio antennae, and you see that on your map. You adjust your map just a bit more so that a straight line from where you think you are on the map, to the radio antennae, continues in a straight line to the actual antennae.

You keep looking at dominant landmarks in all directions, and make slight adjustments to your map so that your map now represents the actual terrain around you.

Now, you can put a few tacks or rocks on your map to keep it secure as long as you stay at your camp. Now study the map.

ALIGNING YOUR MAP WITH THE COMPASS

We'll cover that in the next chapter.

AN AERIAL POINT OF VIEW

Remember, looking at the map is akin to flying by in a small Cesna or drone, and looking down at the terrain. The map tells you what's behind that hill where you don't have a clear view of sight. Your initial task is simply to get that map lined up with the actual terrain.

Study the map and learn the landscapes where the roads and trails go. Is your imaginary path crossing the elevation lines as you travel, or are you staying within the lines? Staying within the lines means your journey is more level. Are there cabins deep in the woods or hills where you might be traveling? If you're lost—or very confused—the map should help you get out, or at least help you get some help.

Roads will always lead to civilization, but rivers don't necessarily. In the back country, once you understand the codes that the mapmakers use, you'll spot graveyards, mines, campgrounds, gravel pits, archaeological sites, forest stations, and much more. The map will show you lakes, rivers, streams, seasonal trickles, springs, water towers, and marsh areas.

Note the year your topographical map was made, since they are not updated annually. Your map might be ten, twenty years old! If there were some updates since the previous version, they will be printed in purple.

Development and population increases result in many more roads, trails, tourist destinations, and even little towns that might not be on your map. On the flip side, buildings, trails, railroad lines, schools, and the like that are shown on the map you're using might not even be present when you're using the map. Yes, besides the great value of having that map, you have to keep in mind that change is persistent and ever-evolving.

USING YOUR MAP TO GET SOMEWHERE

Even without a compass, you can get to a destination with just your map. You know where you are on the map, and you've determined where you want to go. Your map must be aligned with the terrain.

You want to get to a small campground with the table and little stream. It's located about half the map distance from your current location, and it is exactly 90 degrees from your current location. You know it is 90 degrees not because you have a compass (you don't), but because it's exactly in a horizontal line to the right of where you're located.

The easy way to get there is to sight along that line on your map, from where you are to where you want to go, and extended to the east. Then, you have to line up two trees in an exact line, or any two objects in an exact line, and follow them. If you're able to walk flat, in a straight line without obstacles, just keep lining up two objects and following them.

Remember, once you pick up your map from the table and start walking, your map is less useful unless you stop and realign it visually with the terrain.

If everything went well without a hitch, you should arrive at this little campsite in a few hours.

But is there a way to figure how far exactly each increment of the map equals, and how long that increment will take to travel?

FIGURING PACING DISTANCES

To figure distances using your map, you need to know on which scale the map was made. To determine how long it will take you to walk a certain charted course, you should know the length of your own pace.

To determine your pace, go to a place where you know the length of a given distance. This could be a football field, or you can just take a measuring tape and mark a distance on a flat area. A good distance for determining your pace is one hundred feet.

With both feet at the beginning point, step forward with your right foot, then your left foot. That's one. Step forward with the right, then the left, that's two. Continue this way for the full one hundred feet, and note how many paces you made. Now do it again. Note how many paces you took. Divide the paces by one hundred feet and that's your pace.

A pace is a double-step. An average step of thirty inches means a pace of sixty inches, or five feet.

When I walked one hundred feet, I counted twenty-one paces. One hundred feet is 1,200 inches, so I divided 1,200 into forty-two, and learned that my pace is 28.5 inches. It's not a good round number, but that's my pace.

If I have determined (from my map) that I need to walk two miles to my destination, I can do some math before starting out to determine how many paces that will be. A mile is 63,360 inches, so 63,360 x 2 = 126,720 inches to my destination. My pace is sixty inches. Check your calculator: 126,720 divided by 60 is 2,112 paces. That's a lot of paces, and so if you're going to be counting paces, you'll also need some method for keeping track.

It is important to note pace changes on terrain.

- As you move uphill, your pace shortens.
- As you move downhill, your pace lengthens.
- Heavy loads on your back will typically shorten a pace.
- Heavy brush will shorten a pace.

Walking in the wild for any distance will impact the accuracy of your pace count as you navigate obstacles and hills and experience fatigue.

Pacing is probably best for shorter distances, and may not be the most desirable way to keep track of distance, since there are so many variables (including distractions over long periods of time) that will affect your calculations.

Still, this is a skill worth knowing. Many soldiers from both Vietnam and the Middle East have reported how keeping track of their paces was a key factor in their general navigation, coupled with other awareness skills.

QUIZ:

1. True North is at the top of every map. True or False?
2. A map of the terrain could consist entirely of words, with no pictures. True or False?

ANSWERS:

1. False. Some local maps place other directions at the top, for various reasons. But all "official" topographical maps will have True North at the top.
2. True. Why not?

ACTION

Set up a shadow stick, and determine north from the shadows. Align a map with the terrain based on your calculations from the shadow stick.

CHAPTER FIVE

THE COMPASS

What exactly is a compass?

In its simplest form, a compass is nothing more than a magnetized sliver of metal, allowed to spin freely, so that the magnetized end will point to Magnetic North. Have you seen the movie *The Edge*? A plane crashes with rich businessman Anthony Hopkins, along with two other men. Hopkins is city sophisticate, without much of outdoor experience. However, he reads a lot, so his intellectual knowledge is vast. He knows how to make a crude compass. He stroked a little needle with a knife so it would be magnetized, pushed the needle into a leaf and set it into some water where it floated. The needle in the leaf

An early style of compass. A magnet secured to the bottom of the round disk, which is balanced on a pin, causes the disk to point to Magnetic North.

rotated until the tip pointed more or less north. Yes, it was a crude compass, probably somewhat similar to the very first compasses, and though it was very imprecise, it was quite useful.

Historians believe that the very first compasses were just slightly more complex than the little compass made in the film. The very first ones were likely used on ships to help the sailors navigate the seas and oceans, along with star observations.

COMPASS PARTS

Modern compasses give you much more than a needle and a leaf. Still, some are so simplistic that they are not worth your money. Some are very complicated, and cost much more than your need for simply a reliable compass. For our purposes here, I suggest you obtain an orienteering compass, also known as a base plate-style compass. Though there are several companies of manufacture, I suggest Suunto or Silva.

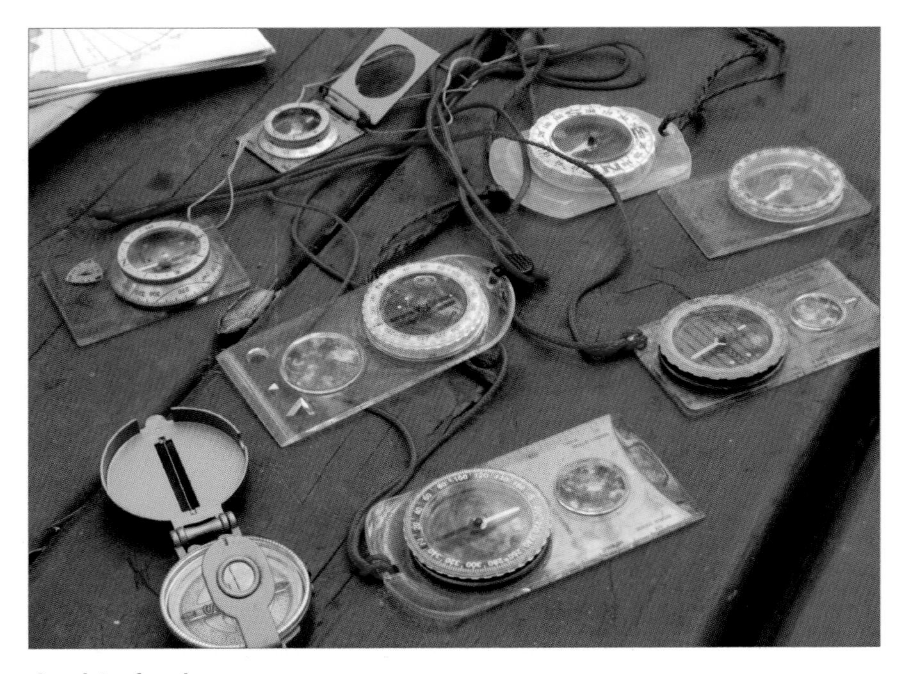

A variety of modern compasses

Look at the picture of an orienteering compass. Get to know the names for its parts:

THE PARTS OF A COMPASS

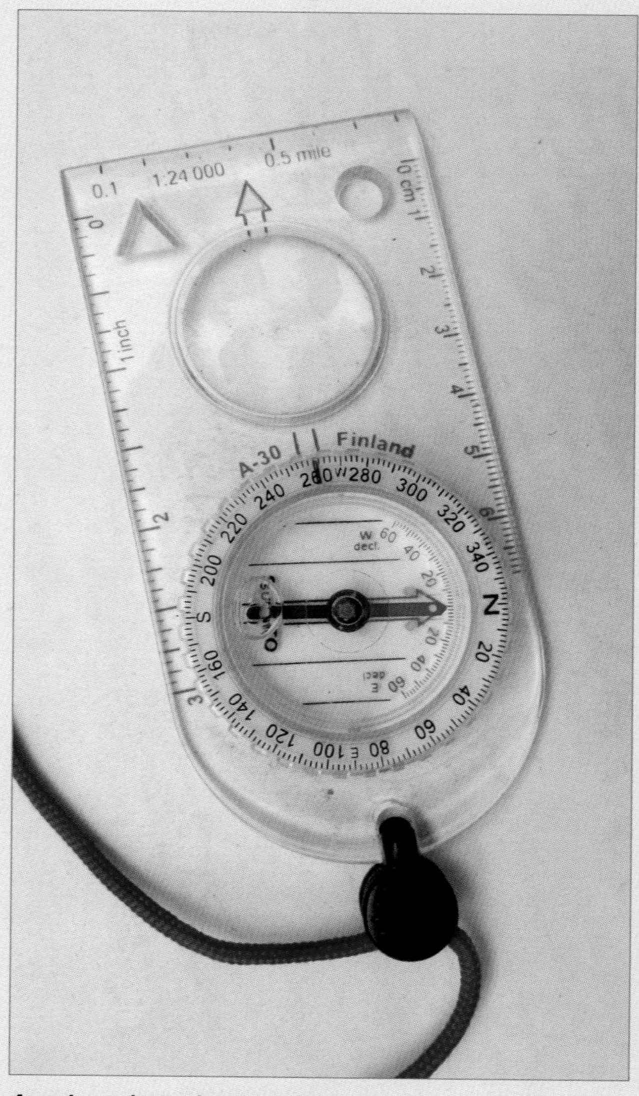

A modern orienteering compass.

The housing: The rectangular plastic base of the compass upon which is printed the "direction of travel" arrow.

The direction of travel arrow: The printed arrow on the housing which you point in the direction you intend to travel.

The dial: The round dial with the printed arrow (the "house"), which turns when you turn the dial. The outer edge of the dial is printed with 360-degree increments.

The needle: The magnetic needle that always points to Magnetic North (the "dog").

There may be other features on the compass you own, such as a mirror or sighting line, and so you should read whatever instructions come with the compass you buy so that you understand all of your compass's features.

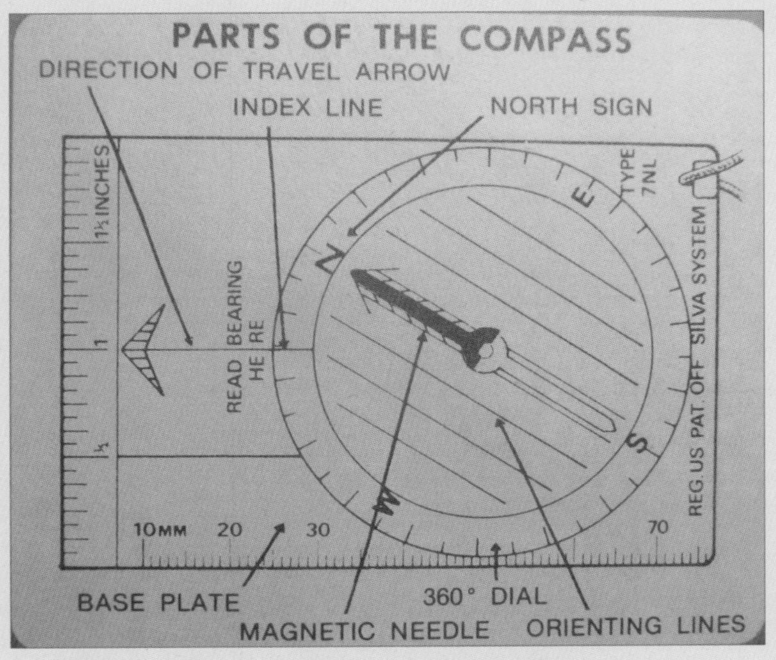

A diagram of the parts of a modern orienteering compass.

PUTTING THE DOG IN THE HOUSE

Now that you have a basic understanding of the compass, let's get somewhere. In this case, let's assume that you want to go about four miles a bit west of south. Your path is somewhat unencumbered through forest, and you're able to walk in more or less a straight line. There are a few hills on the path, and at least two dips. You can actually see a distant lookout tower on the hill where you're heading.

Take your compass and lay it on the palm of your hand, away from metal objects which may inhibit the accuracy of the compass. Using your Direction of Travel arrow, point it directly at the lookout tower. Next, rotate the dial of your compass so that you place the printed arrow directly under the magnetized needle. Remember, the dog is the needle and the printed arrow is the house, so you've just put the dog in the doghouse.

Francisco Loaiza takes a bearing with his compass.

The dog is in the doghouse. The magnetic needle's north end is within the boundaries of the printed arrow on the movable dial of the compass.

WALKING IN A LINE AND RETURNING

Now you can start walking in the direction of the lookout tower, which is where your direction of travel arrow is pointing. As long as you keep the dog in the doghouse, and follow the direction of travel arrow, you will walk straight to the lookout tower. And if you read the point of the 360 degree dial that lines up with the direction of travel arrow, you'll see that you're walking at 200 degrees.

Don't turn your dial—just keep walking. The trip might take longer than you expected, and perhaps fog rolls in and you can't see the lookout tower. Keep walking at 200 degrees. Finally, you get to the lookout tower, you do what you need to do there, and have a lunch. By the time you're ready to return to your starting point, it's gotten dark.

What do you do to the compass now that you're about to return home? Don't touch that dial! While holding the compass flat, simply turn your entire body so that the "south end" of the needle—typically white or black—is superimposed over the printed arrow, the "house." You're going to be returning the exact way you came, so there's no need whatsoever to adjust the compass. Just put the south end of the needle where the north end goes, and follow your Direction of Travel arrow until you get back to your starting point and your car.

If it was daytime, you'd probably be able to see where you started, but now it's nighttime. And every now and then, your path will dip down so you can't see where you're going. Just trust your instrument. Keep the south end of the needle in the doghouse, follow the Direction of Travel arrow, and you'll get home.

DECLINATION

You'll want an understanding of declination (the difference between True North and Magnetic North) and its effect on navigation. We'll cover that in the next chapter.

WHY ARE THERE 360 DEGREES IN A CIRCLE?

As far as we know, this system of dividing a circle into 360 units of measurement, or degrees, comes to us from the ancient Sumerians, and is not based on any organic measurement, except possibly—and this is just speculation—the fact that the year has 365 days. Some ancient societies divided the year into 360 days plus a five-day special period of celebration.

Another organic possibility is that when you take the period of time for each moon—twenty-eight days—and multiply by the number of moons needed to coincide with the solar year—thirteen—you more or less get 365 days. There are a few other speculative possibilities as to why the circle was divided into 360 degrees, but—like it or not—that's the system we've all agreed to use in mathematics.

Thus, when we read a direction as a degree, North is 0, or 360; East is 90; South is 180; and West is 270.

If you're walking at 90 degrees, you're walking due east. Simple. And though some people like to say things like, "We're traveling east-southeast," it's far more precise (and simpler) to use a degree number designation.

CHARTING A COURSE USING A COMPASS ALONE

The PAUL Method

Navigation is a good skill to have and to develop. The use of the map and compass to find one's way through unknown territory is a skill that will never go out of style.

Wait, you say! What about all the apps on smart phones and GPS devices that seemingly render the map and compass obsolete? Modern technology is good, but you still need your device in hand, and it must be working properly.

Knowledge of using your map and compass will always serve you well. But keep in mind that it's impossible to have a map for every single place where you might find yourself. It's easy to carry the compass, and most people only buy maps for the areas where they live and travel regularly. So how useful is just the compass alone?

COMPASS ONLY

Using only your compass, there is a way to keep track of your day's travels, and then to chart the most direct way back to your camp or vehicle. You can use this method when it is daylight, night, or cloudy. You can use it in hilly or flat territory, although it works better in flat territory. It's not that difficult, but it does require a compass, a pen and notebook, and a watch (or some way to keep track of the time).

Now, before we get too far along, let's review (for you beginners) the parts of the compass. (See illustration on page 96.)

This method requires you to record in your notebook your degree of travel of each leg of your journey, and how long you walked. So, how do you determine the degree you are walking?

With your orienteering compass, point the direction-of-travel arrow—which is the printed arrow on the housing of the compass—in the direction you are traveling. So far so good? Now, you turn the round dial until the printed arrow is directly over the north end of the needle. Okay? That's pretty basic compass use. Sometimes we refer to that step as putting the dog in the house. The printed arrow looks a bit like a dog house, and the magnetic needle (the "dog") must be kept aligned with the "doghouse." As long as you keep the dog in the house, and follow your direction-of-travel arrow, you're accurately traveling at whatever degree you've decided to walk in. Then, to know the degree you're walking, you simply look at the number on your compass that corresponds with the "direction of travel" arrow, okay? Simple!

Let's give this a try.

Let's say you've driven to a remote area in the forest and you want to explore the surrounding area all afternoon for herbs, archaeological sites, water, and possible campsites. You set out at 260 degrees, and you walk for ten minutes. You make two columns in your notebook, and you record 260 in the degrees column, and you record ten in the time column.

Francisco Loaiza gets started on his journey with his compass and notebook.

The notation in the notebook shows that Loaiza has walked ten minutes at 260 degrees.

After walking for ten minutes at 260 degrees, this is recorded in the notebook.

Then, you decide to change directions, and you head out at 140 degrees. You write that down in the "degrees" column. You walk for

Loaiza continues on his journey, in a different direction.

After walking thirty minutes at 140 degrees, this is recorded in the notebook.

Loaiza checks his notes before heading out again.

thirty minutes before you pause, so you record thirty in the minutes column.

With another direction change, Loaiza continues.

After walking forty minutes at 60 degrees, this is recorded in the notebook.

He continues walking. After walking ten minutes at 100 degrees, this is recorded in the notebook.

Loaiza continues in another direction.

After walking for thirty minutes at 330 degrees, Loaiza takes a rest and records the details in his notebook.

Loaiza has decided that he's done hiking for the day. Now he's going to find the shortest way back to where he started.

You continue this way for the rest of the day, always recording the degree in which you walked, and the amount of time you walked in that direction.

In order for this system to work optimally, you need to walk in fairly straight lines during each leg of your journey. In extremely rugged terrain, this system might not be practical or possible. If one leg of your journey was uphill and you had to walk more slowly, you should make a note of that. If you had to slow down to cross a stream, you should make a note of that. Where a downhill route means you covered more territory more rapidly, make a note of it.

Let's now review your note and attempt to create a map from them. Let's say you're done exploring for the day, and your notebook contains five entries for degree traveled, and five entries for amount of time traveled.

With that information, you are now going to create a simple map to determine a straight path back to your camp or wherever you started from.

Let's take a look at the notes you took, in the example, and let's create a map.

Here is an example of what your notes might look like.

DEGREE of TRAVEL	TIME TRAVELED
260	10
140	30
60	40
100	10
330	30

Remember, this is just an example, and in the example, we have kept the units of time all divisible by ten minutes. In real life, your units of time would likely be much more diverse.

Using your notebook or sticks on the ground, you will turn the units of time into linear lengths. So, for example, each ten minutes of time traveled will be equal to one inch. It doesn't really matter whether you make each ten minute segment represent one inch or five inches or the length of your finger or the length of your Swiss army knife—just be consistent with whatever unit of conversion you use.

So let's say you are going to use sticks to create a map. For your first ten-minute leg of your journey, you cut a straight stick one inch long (ten minutes = one inch). Lay the stick on the ground and align it at 260 degrees, your direction of travel.

Your next leg of your journey was thirty minutes, at 140 degrees. So you cut a stick that is three inches long. From the leading end of the first stick, set down your three inch long stick and align it at 140 degrees. So far so good? You are creating a map of your journey.

Next, you cut a four inch stick and align it at the end of the last stick at 60 degrees.

Next, cut another one inch stick and align it at 100 degrees from the end of the last stick.

Finally, you cut a stick three inches (thirty minutes = three inches) and set it at the end of the last stick at 330 degrees.

Okay? You have just created a visual map of your journey using sticks, converting time into linear lengths. When you have completed your stick-map, you now place your compass at the end of the last stick (which represents where you stopped, and decided you wanted to go home), and point it to your starting point. That is your direct line

A stick map has been created based on the notes kept, for time traveled and angle traveled. Each stick is laid out according to the angle traveled, and its length corresponds to the time traveled.

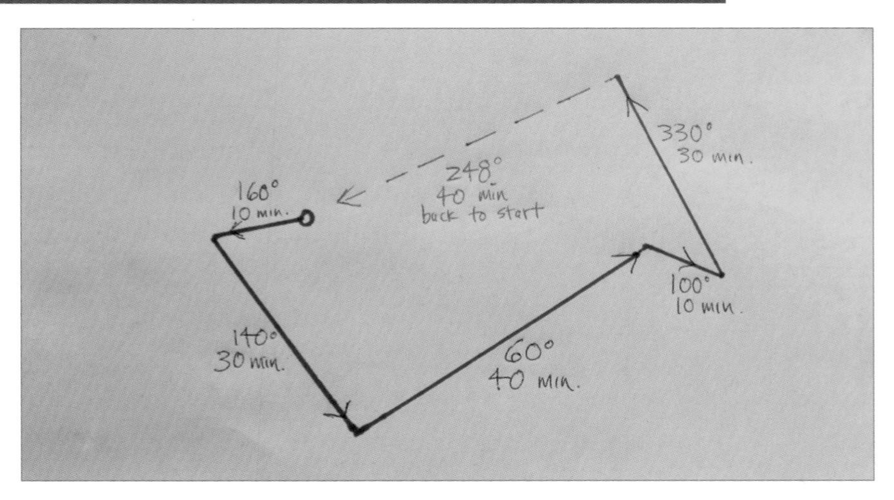

A schematic showing the angles traveled, and how to figure the way back.

back to your camp. Put the dog in the house on your compass, and simply follow the direction of travel arrow back home!

Because you have chosen each ten minutes of travel time to represent one inch, you can just measure your straight line back to your camp to get a good idea of how long it will take you to get back to your camp or car.

From my reckoning, it appears that you can now walk straight at 248 degrees, for about forty minutes and you'll be back in your camp! Not bad, considering that your entire journey so far took two hours.

Now, let's again discuss the variables that come with uneven terrain. For example, if you had a lot of uphill travel, you probably couldn't cover as much terrain in ten minutes as you could if the ground were flat. So you should record these terrain changes in your notebook. If you walked for twenty minutes, it would normally represent a two-inch stick. But if the terrain was very sharply uphill, you wouldn't have been able to cover the same distance in the same time. You would estimate, and probably use just a one inch stick for that leg of your journey.

You should also record any changes in the speed of your hiking, though this system works best if your speed is more or less the same.

So, using our example, you now walk back looking for your camp. You walk at 248 degrees for the estimated forty minutes. Whoa! You didn't end up in your camp! Now what? First, don't panic. Remember, you had some ups and downs in your day's journey, and it all didn't relate perfectly to dimensions of the stick map you made. Perhaps there is some prominent feature that might make your camp recognizable. Can you get to a high point (like up a tree) and see if the camp is visible?

You can't recognize anything as your camp, so here's what you do. First, mark where you ended up somehow. Make a pile of stones, or tie a cord around a tree, or something so you know where you ended. Hopefully, you won't come back to this point.

Now, begin to make a clockwise circle around this point. Be very observant. Keep circling around and around, making a slightly bigger circle each time. Eventually, you should find your camp.

If you don't like the looseness of continually making a larger circle, try making squares. Walk ten paces north from your ending point, then ten paces east, then twenty paces south, twenty paces west, thirty paces north, thirty paces east, forty paces south, etc., always continually expanding your area. Unless you made some very serious errors in the recording of the legs of your journey, you will soon find your camp.

There's a bit more to this, so please come to one of my Orienteering workshops when you can. Also, get a copy of each of these following books:

- *The Green Beret's Compass Course* by Don Paul. The technique described in this section was based on his book.
- *Be Expert with Map and Compass* by Björn Kjellström is still one of the best overall guides to map and compass use.
- *How to Survive Anywhere* by Christopher Nyerges includes a short section on navigation.
- Ron Hood's NAVIGATION video [volume 4 of his WoodMaster's series] from www.Survival.com.

GETTING AROUND OBJECTS USING YOUR COMPASS

Remember, to master the art of orienteering, you should enroll in a college-level course in land navigation, or join an orienteering club near you. There are many more ways to navigate the landscape using your map and compass.

Here's a way to get around obstacles you might encounter, using all of the skills you've learned so far in this book.

In this example, we'll keep it simple.

You're traveling east to your destination, which means that you are traveling at 90 degrees. (East is 90, South is 180, West is 270, and North is 0 or 360 degrees.)

You come to a large obstacle, which you obviously need to go around. Your goal is to get around that obstacle and then get back on your route, traveling 90 degrees.

You can go around that obstacle by walking three parts of a square, or by walking two parts of a triangle. This will be very simple geometry, but look at the pictures too, because some folks get very confused by this.

THE SQUARE

To get around your obstacle, you will need to make a 90-degree right turn and count your paces. Then when you think you have cleared the obstacle, you make another turn, to your left at 90 degrees. You walk until you have cleared the obstacle and it's not necessary to count paces here.

Once you've cleared the obstacle, now you turn left again 90 degrees, and count your paces. Go the same number of paces that you traveled at the first leg of your detour. Okay?

When you're done pacing, you are now back in line with your original line of travel. Turn right 90 degrees and continue on your way.

It doesn't matter what direction you were originally traveling when you do this. Just make the right turn, left turn, and left turn, all 90-degree angles, and get back to your original path.

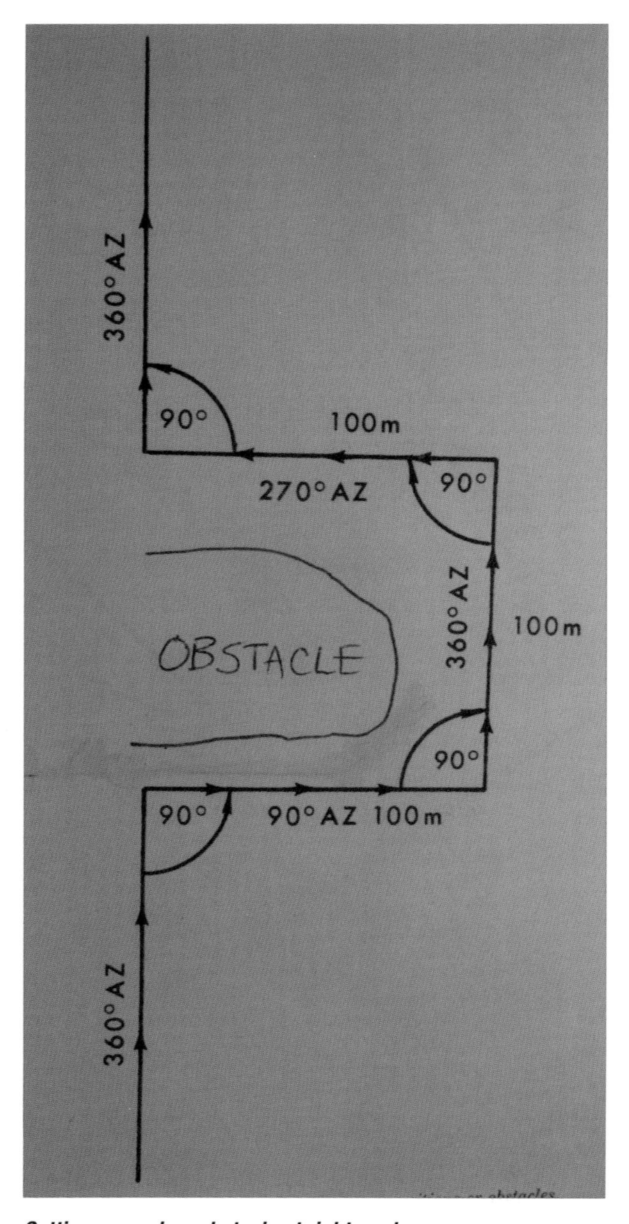

Getting around an obstacle at right angles.

THE TRIANGLE

You come to an obstacle, and you've again been traveling east, or 90 degrees. This time you decide that a triangle detour is best. You can move around an obstacle as we did above, but this time you can walk on two sides of a triangle, rather than three sides of a square.

Remember: three inside corners of an equilateral triangle each measure 60 degrees. Three inside angles times 60, equals 180 degrees. There are always 180 degrees of angles inside any triangle. An equilateral triangle is easiest to figure, and you should probably stick to that if you're in the field. No need to create even greater confusion with an odd isosceles triangle.

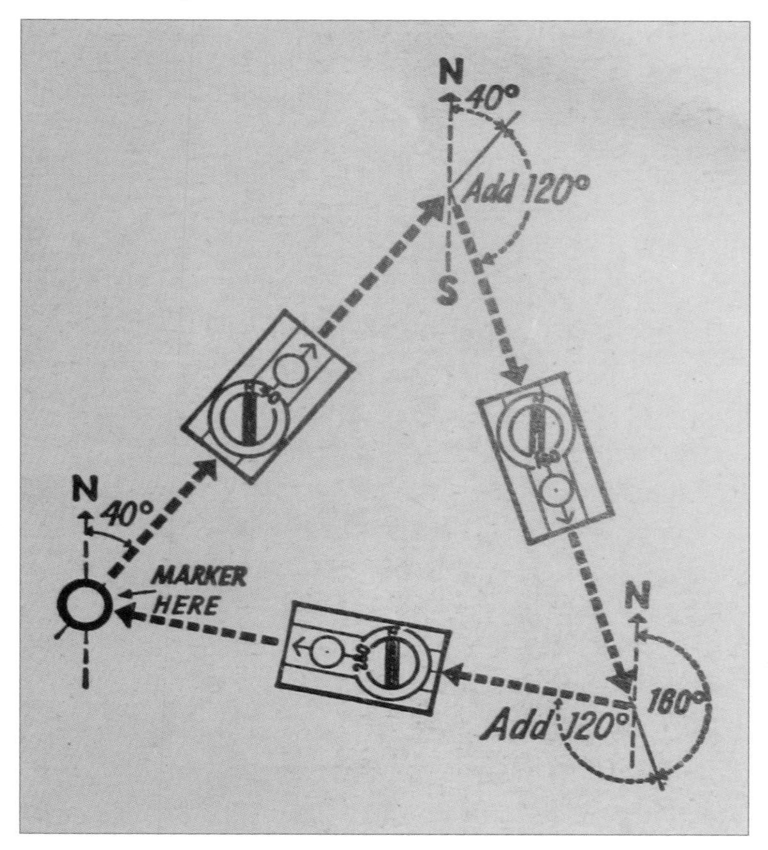

An example of how to go around an obstacle on two sides, or how to get back to where you started with a large triangle.

COMPASSES TO AVOID

Your compass should be a simple workhorse. It doesn't matter if it impresses your friends or not. It has to be easy to use and you need to know how to use it.

In the purest form, anything can be called a compass if it has a magnetic needle and the cardinal points printed around the circle.

The little compasses that you attach to your zipper pulls are clever, but not very useful.

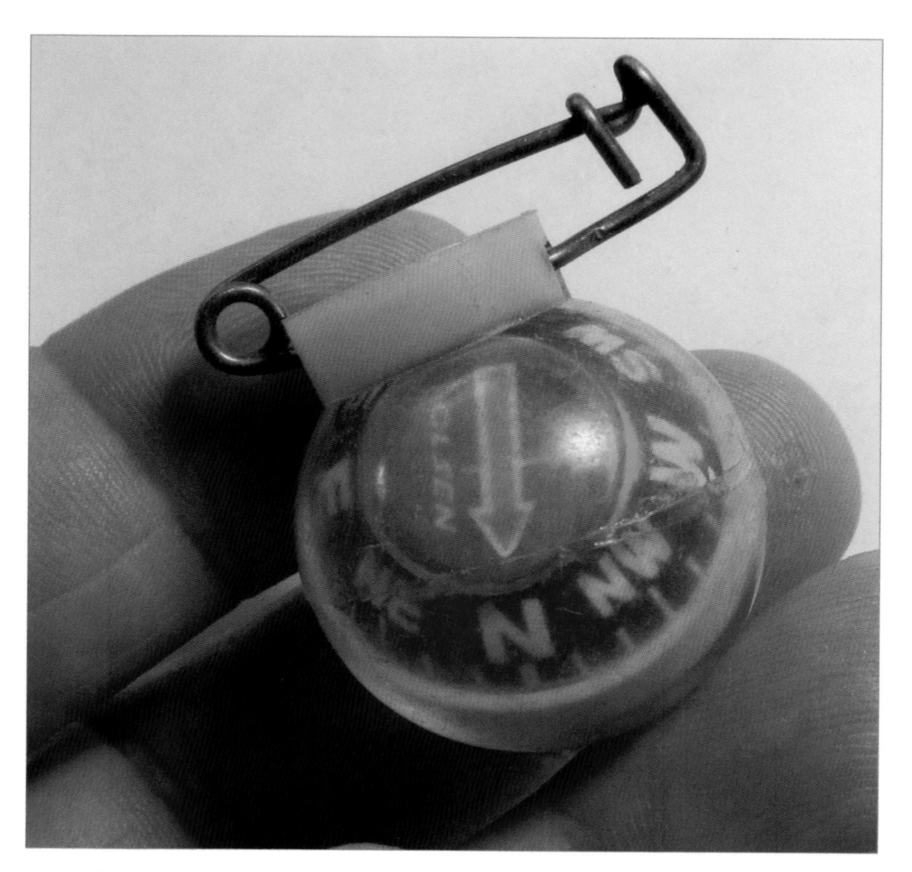

These little pin-on compasses—and similar compasses which cannot be calibrated and which have no direction of travel arrow—are of very limited usefulness.

A simple compass on the butt of a knife—such as the one pictured—is of almost no value because no adjustments or references can be made.

The little round ball compasses that pin to your fishing vest are likewise of limited value. I suppose they are intended to announce to all who see it that "Hey, I'm a guy who knows where I'm going," but, in fact, such a compass is of hardly any practical value because no adjustments can be made and there is no such thing as keeping the dog in the dog house.

Remember the once-popular Rambo knives? They usually had a small round compass attached to the end of the rather fat, round, and hollow handle. Again, this compass had a magnetized needle, and the printed cardinal points, but it was of limited use as a workhorse.

QUIZ:

1. The magnetic end of your compass's needle points to the North Pole. True or False?
2. If you're in the southern hemisphere, you need to buy a special compass that points to the South Pole. True or False?

ANSWERS

1. False. It points to Magnetic North.
2. False.

ACTION

In a large open field, mark where you are standing. Point the "direction of travel" arrow of your compass at a distant point. With your compass, "put the dog in the doghouse." Walk to your distant point following your direction of travel arrow. You can count your steps, or not. When you reach your destination, turn around, and put the opposite end of the compass needle in the doghouse. Do not turn the dial. Follow the direction of travel arrow. If you counted your steps, count again. You should end up on your beginning mark.

"Whether or not we humans have a magnetic sense of direction, magnetic fields are known to affect rabbits, mice, and rats, and influence the heart rate and function of monkeys. There is even anecdotal evidence to suggest that magnetic storms have some bearing on psychiatric conditions in humans and even possibly raise the incidence of suicides. An interesting picture of the relationship between all animals, including humans, and magnetism is building, but it is very far from complete."

—Tristan Gooley, *The Natural Navigator*

CHAPTER SIX

USING THE MAP AND COMPASS TOGETHER

A compass certainly makes the map more useful.

Here are some of things you can now do a bit easier using the map and compass together.

- Find the shortest route to a particular point.
- Find the easiest route to a particular point.
- Find the easiest way around a mountain.
- Chart a course to an unseen destination.
- Chart a course that passes through differing environments.
- Find the best route that allows you to stay on the highest terrain.
- Choose a hiking route that allows you to avoid as much contact with "civilization" as possible.
- Go directly to a campsite.
- Go directly to water sources.
- Go directly to a specific structure.
- Chart a safe cross-country, off-trail course.
- Create challenging games with youth groups.

Yes, you can do some of these listed tasks with only your map or only your compass, but you can do all of them easier by using the map and compass together as a unit.

Your most important initial task may be to align your map with the actual terrain. You can pick up your map and compass and hike along your way, and then, if you're a bit confused, pull out your map, adjust it to the terrain, and examine your surroundings to see if you're still on track.

Once you're synergistically using your map and compass together, this can be a very easy process to stay on track.

ALIGNING YOUR MAP WITH THE TERRAIN WHILE USING YOUR COMPASS

Let's begin with the simple map alignment.

There are a few ways to do this. Remember, the goal is to have your map aligned with the territory.

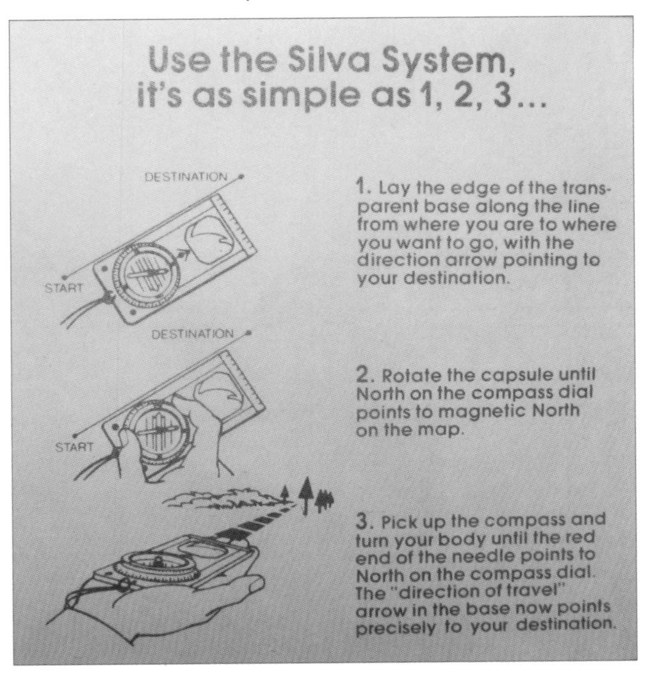

A very basic way of aligning your map with your compass. Courtesy of Silva.

One of the most common ways to do this is to first lay the edge of the transparent base of your compass housing along the line on your map from where you are to where you want to go. This means that the direction of travel arrow will be pointing to your destination (on the map).

Next, rotate the round dial until north on the dial points to Magnetic North on the map. True North is at the top of your map, but Magnetic North is determined by looking at the little triangular image at the bottom of your map which shows you the relative location of True North (Grid North), and Magnetic North. (See illustration.) In other words, the red printed arrow on the dial must be parallel with the Magnetic North line.

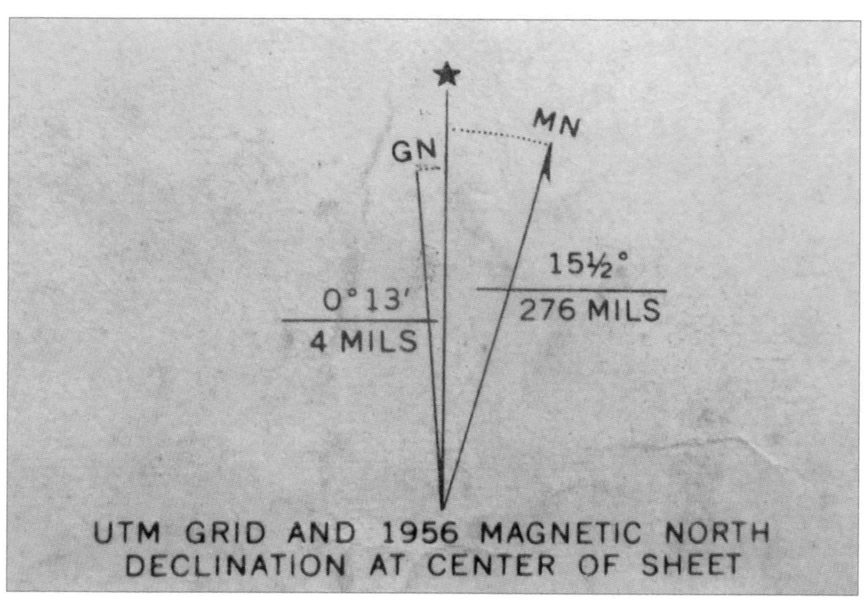

A symbol found on all topographical maps which shows you the difference between True North and Magnetic North; that difference is referred to as declination.

Finally, pick up your compass and without touching the compass dial, just turn your body until the magnetic needle points to the north on the dial. In most cases, this means that your needle will be directly in line with the red printed arrow which points north.

Once these are aligned, the direction of travel arrow is now pointing directly to your destination. As long as you "keep the dog in the house" (as discussed in a previous chapter, page 83), you'll be able to walk straight to your destination.

WHAT IS DECLINATION?

MAGNETIC NORTH VS. TRUE NORTH

It's important to be clear about the difference between Magnetic North vs. True North.

When you look at that globe of the earth in your classroom, note how the earth is spinning on its axis. That point at the north is called the North Pole, also known as True North.

The North Pole is the true physical top-most point or zone of the earth.

But your compass doesn't point there, usually. For reasons that are sometimes debated, compasses point to a zone roughly northwest of Hudson Bay. This magnetic zone is not fixed, and in fact, its movement is charted. However, its deviation is so slight from year to year that we can assume for practical purposes that this is a more or less fixed zone where compasses point, which we call Magnetic North.

Why does your compass needle point there? Scientists who study the inner workings of the earth believe that the movement of molten iron in the Earth's core acts like a giant generator and creates the magnetic forces of Earth. Jeremy Bloxham, a Harvard geophysicist, stated that according to his research, most of the forces of the magnetic field exit from the inner core through two cold spots in the rocky mantle beneath the Antarctic continent. These forces then loop northward across the planet, and re-enter the core through two more cold spots in the Earth's mantle, one beneath Northern Canada and another in Siberia.

Bloxham explained the mechanics of this motion in a report in the British journal, *Nature.*

Scientists who map the magnetic field of the earth point out that the Magnetic North is not static, but changes about a tenth of a degree every year. Still, the magnetic North Pole is static enough so that during our lifetimes, our compasses can be a reliable tool for navigation.

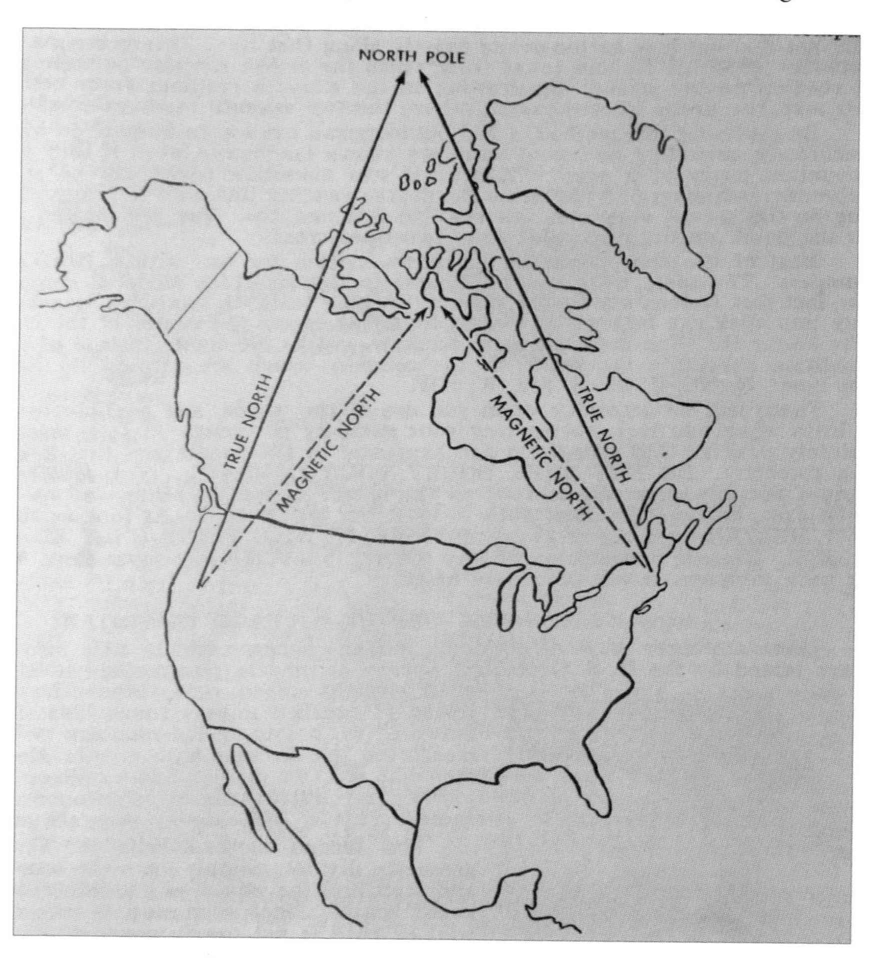

A map of the US and Canada, showing where compasses point (Magnetic North) vs. the True North.

It is important to remember that declination is used when pairing a map and compass together. Its purpose is to correctly align the map with the territory. In other words, one can think of declination adjustment as a translator, so that a map and compass can work together.

If you're using only a map, or only a compass, then declination is not important.

The reason we adjust for declination is because of the magnetic forces at play on the earth. These forces don't always correspond with True North. To correct for this deviation when using a compass, look for the declination written into the legend of the map. Sometimes maps have a little diagram showing declination, sometimes it is simply written. So, to correct for these subtle deviations, called declination, we have to make adjustments.

One supposedly "simple" way is to remember is that we read from left to right. We also associate moving in a direction from left to right as forward, or best, while moving left as regressive, back or least.

WEST IS BEST, EAST IS LEAST

If we remember the Boy Scout slogan— "West is Best, East is Least" —we have a simple tool for adjusting the compass for declination. If you're on the West Coast, you turn the dial in a clockwise—to the right—direction. When on the East Coast, turn the dial counter-clockwise—to the left—direction. How much you turn depends on the amount of declination the map indicates.

The boundary line—0 degrees between True North and Magnetic North—runs from Canada south through eastern Wisconsin and eastern Illinois, south through western Kentucky and Tennessee, through Alabama and through Florida's panhandle, down in a southeasterly direction in the Gulf of Mexico. Along that line, there is negligible difference between True North and Magnetic North.

If you live to the east of that line—the Least—you turn your compass dial counterclockwise (which adds degrees).

If you live to the west of that line—the Best—you turn your compass dial clockwise (which subtracts degrees).

It's that simple! Simple, except I usually cannot remember this very simple technique, so I usually lay my compass on the map, as already

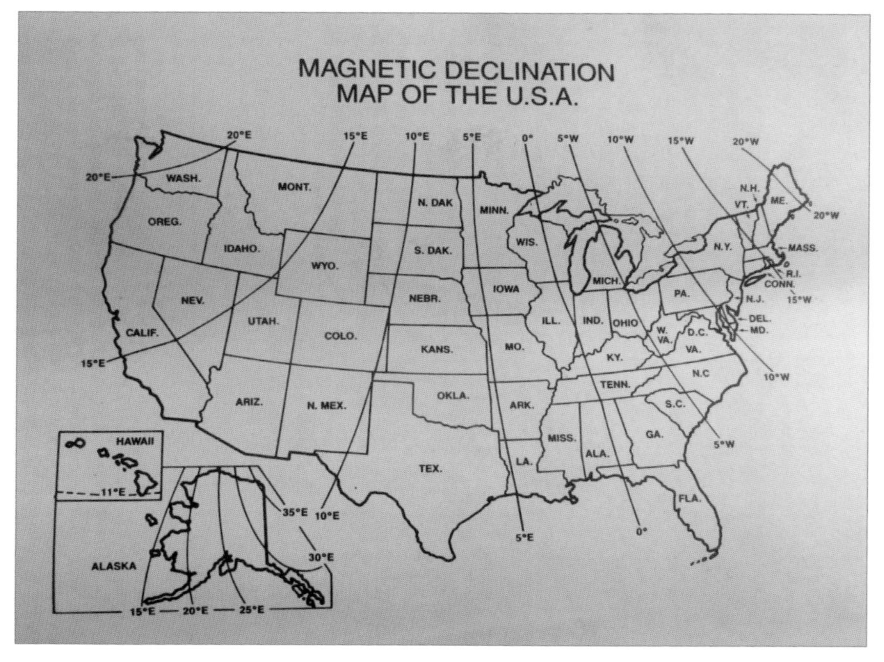

A map for the United States showing the magnetic declination for each area.

described, so that the compass needle is parallel to the Magnetic North line of declination code.

On a typical baseplate compass, each little vertical black line is called a tick line and is representative of two degrees. So, if you live in Los Angeles and our map indicates a declination of 12 degrees easterly declination, you turn the dial CLOCKWISE—to the right— six tick marks worth which would equal 12 degrees.

SIMPLE ON-THE-FLY METHOD

There are several methods of syncing the map and compass together, but by far, the simplest, on-the-fly method is:

1. Lay the map flat on the ground.
2. Adjust the compass for declination.

3. Lay the baseplate of the compass, in perfect alignment, along one of the long straight black edges along the sides of the map, left or right doesn't matter.
4. Rotate the entire map, while the compass is still laying on the map, until the compass needle is flush inside the dog house.

Congratulations! Your map is now accurately oriented to the territory.

It is important the map not move from this position while taking or transferring bearings. Placing small stones on all four corners of the map once it is oriented works well to keep it from moving. If the map is accidentally moved, one will have to reset it by using steps 1 through 4 above.

EXERCISES

Common Boy Scout and Orienteering exercises help you to hone your navigational skills.

There are far more ways in which to navigate and practice orienteering than this book could cover. There are specialized workbooks, and courses, to practice those skills.

Check out this site: https://www.scoutshop.org/beginners-compass-game-600893.html

This is where you can buy two of the Boy Scouts of America's games for honing your compass skills.

Beginners Compass Game, product number 600893, is an excellent game for both the beginner and advanced compass user. With this game, a course is laid out with eight points on a circle as large as you wish. Beginning at one spot, the participant walks to four more points following a compass bearing, and then checks to see if they got it right. This game has ninety combinations.

Compass Game, product number 600894, is another game to improve your skills. This one is based upon a fifty-foot line, where the participant follows several compass bearings and paces out specific distances, so you need to know your pace before you start.

A Field Experience with Map and Compass

Many years ago—I was still in my twenties—the non-profit organization I was working with received a phone call from someone wanting to know if we would do some claim-staking. The man wanted to hire someone to stake mineral claims on some federal land east of Lake Isabel. We had a long discussion, and finally, Timothy Hall and I had a meeting to discuss the job.

We learned that "staking a claim" means just that! We had to haul 2x4s on our backs, and place those stakes in the field at specified points. At our new employer's office, we were shown aerial photographs of the property, and our job was going to be to define huge rectangles by placing one 2x4 at each corner, and also one 2x4 inside each rectangle, where we were to place a notice stating who was staking the claim. These rectangles were huge, measuring, twenty-five by one hundred yards! The terrain was steep, and wooded. There were sixteen of these rectangles to be staked and claimed. Fortunately, at least some were side by side so one stake would help to define at least two rectangles.

Our new employer actually gave us a huge chain, which he thought we could use to measure the rectangles. We were also given local topographical maps with dots where we were to place our 2x4s.

When we got to the field, the rough, wooded nature of the terrain made hauling a chain around highly impractical. Instead, we located each of our dots by using our map and compass, using a method known as triangulation.

We began our work by walking to one of the points on the map that was very easy to locate. We dug a hole and put in a 2x4. Then, we would pace to find the next spot. Both of our paces—on flat ground—measured about 2.5 feet, and this would be shorter when we were going uphill. When we got to the next spot, we stopped, and pulled out our map and compass. Fortunately, even though we were on a hillside, we had a pretty good view of the west and south, with some prominent features. We'd sight a prominent feature, locate that feature on the map, and then draw a pencil line to where we thought we were. We would do this with at least three features, and if the three pencil lines all lined up, then *bingo*, we were on target. If the pencil lines did not line up, we would calculate where we *should* be, move, and then re-figure with the pencil lines.

Although sixteen rectangles might sound like a small job, it took us all of two days and part of a third to get the job done. Timothy and I learned a lot about triangulation because we needed to for this job. In our case, the boss told us that each 2x4 had to be within twenty-five feet of the dot on the map. That meant if we got the 2x4 within a fifty-foot radius, we'd be okay.

The hard part wasn't doing the triangulation—in fact, when we sat to do our figuring, that was the only time we got to rest. Otherwise, this was back-breaking work carrying 2x4s, and walking through dry hillsides covered with miserable fox-tail grasses that cut into our socks and pants. (By the second day, we discovered the value of makeshift gaiters).

After the work was done, we were glad to have gotten a good paycheck, and felt good that after the boss hired someone else to check our work, they were able to confirm that we'd done the job within the set standards.

Also, only until after we were done did I learn how they came to hire us. At that time, Timothy and I were affiliated with the non-profit, one of whose subsidiaries was "The Survival Shop." The man who needed the surveying work done told us that he merely looked into the phone book for "surveyors," but called us because the few surveyors listed weren't interested. We were listed under "survival" next to the surveyors!

But we learned our lessons quickly. I have used the triangulation method several times since, at least one time when I was fairly confused in the Sequoia National Forest—the condition that most call "lost."

FOUR SIMPLE METHODS OF USING A MAP AND COMPASS TOGETHER

ALIGNING THE MAP WITH THE COMPASS

1. Lay the map on a flat table or flat spot.
2. Lay the compass on the map.
3. Turn the compass housing so the grid lines line up with the map's north-south lines.
4. Adjust the compass for declination (in the case of LA County, subtract 15 degrees).
5. Adjust the map (with the compass on it) by turning the map until the magnetic needle lines up with the printed arrow. Now the map is lined up correctly with the natural terrain.

WALKING IN A STRAIGHT LINE

1. Lay the compass on the map.
2. Situate the compass so that "where you are" and "where you want to go" are two points along one edge of the compass.
3. Turn the compass housing so that the grid lines line up with the north-south lines.
4. Adjust for declination.
5. Turn the map (with the compass on it) until the magnetic needle is aligned with the permanent arrow printed on the compass.
6. Pick up the compass and follow the "direction-of-travel" arrow.
7. Walk in a straight line to your destination, always keeping the magnetic needle inside the "direction-of-travel" arrow.

GOING BACK THE EXACT WAY YOU CAME

Follow all of the above, then:

1. Do not turn or adjust the compass housing.
2. Holding the compass in your hand, turn your body until the magnetic needle is pointing to the opposite end of your "direction-of-travel arrow" (i.e. 180 degrees off).
3. Hold the compass in hand, and return from the direction you came.
4. Keep the magnetic needle aligned with the permanent arrow printed on the compass until you reach your destination.

GOING AROUND A LARGE OBSTACLE AND THEN GETTING BACK ON YOUR STRAIGHT COURSE

1. You're traveling east. Let's assume that you'll go around the obstacle by going around to the south.
2. Turn 90 degrees to your right and begin traveling at 180 degrees (south), and then count your paces until you have "cleared" the obstacle.
3. Turn 90 degrees to your left (east) and walk directly east until you have actually gone beyond the obstacle.
4. Now, again turn 90 degrees to your left (which will be north), and now count off the same number of paces you earlier traveled to "clear" the obstacle.
5. When you have walked off all the paces, you should now be back in line with your original direction of travel.
6. Turn 90 degrees to your right (east) and resume your journey in the direction you had been going.

QUIZ:

1. The Magnetic North Pole is a somewhat static fixed point in the vicinity of Hudson Bay. True or False?
2. Using a map that is accurately aligned with your terrain, you are able to find the easiest route to your destination. True or False?
3. Using a map that is accurately aligned with your terrain, you are able to find the most direct path to your destination. True or False?

ANSWERS

1. False. The "Magnetic North pole" actually moves and is not static.
2. True.
3. True.

CHAPTER SEVEN

HOW TO AVOID GETTING LOST

Why do people get lost?

There are countless reasons why people get lost, though we can lump most of these reasons into a few categories.

Often, after a lost person is found, they often say that they simply went out for a walk, didn't plan to stay long, but got disoriented. Sometimes unexpected weather occurs. But because they didn't expect to stay long, the lost person did not bring along even basic supplies that would have helped out tremendously.

And, if you're just out for a casual stroll, you go where you are familiar, comfortable, and where you feel there is no danger of getting mixed up. Therefore, you don't exert the mental exertion to observe the terrain as if your life depended upon these observations.

Sometimes, the lost hiker will venture into an area that they'd only read about, or watched on YouTube. The brief magazine description, or the tantalizing YouTube video, seldom shows any of the dangers, and makes what is often a long and strenuous journey seem as if it is a very short stroll that any child could do.

Another reason for getting lost is that the person is really having a good time. They enjoy each twist and turn in the terrain, and they are marveling at the flowers and insects and vistas. Even if there is a clear trail, trails often fork and then those trails fork into multiple directions. Were you always looking back, especially after each change of direction? Probably not. When you finally decided to head back to your car, you realized that you'd gone a bit further than expected, and somehow the trail now looked different, and before you knew it, you had no idea where you were, or how to find your car.

As you hike along, periodically look back the way you came. Often, an area will look dramatically different when viewed from the opposite side. Here, Angelo Cervera checks the area behind him, where he's just hiked.

Then, there is also the use of drugs and alcohol, which don't help you to maintain your sense of direction in unfamiliar territory. (That's obvious, right?)

It's easy to get lost – in fact, it happens all the time, routinely.

What are some common awareness techniques for not getting lost?

We've all heard that if you get lost (or very confused) in the woods, that you should hug a tree, right? Will that help you find your way? No, it won't! However, the key point is that you STOP and try to figure out where you are.

STOP is the acronym for: Stop, Think, Observe, Plan.

This is where the "hug-a-tree" idea came from. If you're lost, you need to quit getting more lost. If you stayed put and hugged a tree, at least you'd not be getting farther and farther away from wherever it is you should be.

Dorothy Wong "hugs a tree" to demonstrate that you should stay put if you are lost.

Stop: Quit moving. Yes, you're on the verge of panic and you have plans for the evening. You certainly don't want your friends to think that you can't get from point A to point B in the woods. They might laugh at you! However, you only have one goal now. Get un-lost, and survive! Quit moving. Sit down. Hug a tree if need be.

Think: Okay, now that you've stopped, think it all over. How did you get here? Were there turns in the road? Were there signs that you didn't see, or ignored? Did you lose the trail? Is there a spot where you knew the area well, and then after a while, you didn't? Do you recall where that was? Could you backtrack? Can you follow your own tracks? Were you with others? How long ago was it that you parted ways? Think!

Observe: You're hopefully a bit calmer now. Don't move from the tree, but start looking in all directions. You probably know how you got to this tree, and is there anything you can see back beyond where you came from? Do you notice any distant landmarks, such as a high peak, a water tower in the distance, or other landscape features? Is it possible to climb the tree you're sitting under so you can get a better view of your terrain? Were there any sounds that you recall from earlier? Try closing your eyes, cupping your hand behind your ear to amplify the sound, and listen to each area. Slowly, turn a bit and listen again. Turn some more. Hear anything different, new, or familiar?

Plan: It was good that you stopped, took a breath, and attempted to take stock of your surroundings. Now what are you going to do? You could just stay there, and make yourself more visible somehow. Is it safe to make a smoky fire? That might be a good way to make yourself more visible to others, and maybe rescuers. Is it getting cold? Can you make a good shelter to spend the night? Perhaps you decide that you have collected enough facts that you can try to find your way out. You should only push on if you have a fairly good idea of where you need to go. Pull out a notepad and pen and make yourself a map. You probably don't have a compass with you, but if you do, you can at least walk in straight lines rather than meandering here and there.

Finally, you have to put your plan into action. You're going to stay, or you're going to move along. Find a way to leave some sort of trail or sign of your path, just in case someone is out to find you, and is looking for signs that you were there.

DON'T PANIC

In the heat of the emergency, don't panic. Yes, easy to say, harder to implement. If you're operating from a perspective of fear or panic, your decisions will not be the best.

Stop, breathe, and think. If you must act quickly and decisively, let your intuition and your experience guide you.

What's the worst that can happen? Come to think of it, there are a lot of bad things that can and do occur. Focus on solutions and keep a positive attitude.

In this scenario, you're lost, confused, uncertain, and mixed-up.

If moving will just get you more confused, then stop. Fire, smoke, noise, signaling mirrors—any of these might be appropriate ways to draw attention to yourself.

If not, consider finding, or making, a shelter for the night.

With today's technology, there is absolutely no reason one shouldn't carry some sort of Satellite emergency communication device—Resqlink, SPOT, or InReach. Think about this: If it's good enough that the FAA requires all airplanes to have one, why wouldn't you want one for yourself?

The personal devices are a bit different than an airplane model because they are meant to be portable.

Each of the three mentioned devices operates a bit differently, so please do some research and buy the one that fit your needs.

You've decided to leave your camp, but it's possible that someone might come there trying to find you. You should leave a note or some sign that you were there, and where you are going. Yes, a piece of paper is often left on a table or under a rock somewhere, but pieces of paper get blown about in the wind, or destroyed in the rain. Have you ever tried leaving a note on an old beer can?

Cut a square from any aluminum can—yes, you find them practically everywhere. With a stick, scratch your message onto the aluminum. Think about what you want to write, and keep it to the point. You departed your camp on noon Saturday, and you're heading west. Hang that piece of aluminum with a string in a tree where it will be seen. It will flutter around in the wind and be visible, and the rain will not destroy it.

Cutting a rectangular piece from a discarded aluminum can.

Dorothy Wong cuts a piece of aluminum from a discarded can with her Swiss Army knife in order to make an aluminum sign.

You can scratch a note onto a piece of aluminum, and secure it in a bush or tree where someone will see it. The aluminum sign won't blow away, or get destroyed by rain.

Common (bad) habits of people who get lost

"Getting lost" is a state of mind, in a sense. Sometimes you might be hiking along nonchalantly, and then you realize that you're not quite sure where you are, but you're sure you're not lost. You keep going. You look around. You might pause, and you might look behind you. But at some point, you ask yourself. *Where am I*? This becomes a very pressing question in your mind. You might even start to wonder why the sun is setting in the east! (Yes, believe me—that happened to me!)

It's a lot better if you're "lost" with a group than if you're by yourself. Why? More heads are better than one, in this case. If you put everyone's strengths and weaknesses together, there should be enough strengths to help you determine where you went astray, and figure out how to get back on track.

And there are a lot of other really good reasons to go hiking with others. For one thing, it's a lot more enjoyable. And in your small group, keep in mind that people have their natural ups and downs. Most people find it very hard to be "up" and fully alert at every moment. That's why it's better to be with a good group. But if you decided to be a Rambo and head out alone, well, we hope you can be "up" all the time.

But most people can't.

Many modern urban people are so used to noises and distractions that they are very uncomfortable alone by themselves in the relative silence of the outdoors. For this reason, such hikers carry radios so there is some noise to break the silence. You have to wonder why they went into the wilderness in the first place, but that's another issue. If not a radio, it's the ubiquitous "smart" phone, which seems to command constant attention. Whether a radio or phone, these technological devices take our attention away from the details of the trail. These details include the smells, sounds, temperature changes, and changes in terrain—subtle or obvious. Taking note of these details is part of the art of awareness.

On the flip side, if you do have your smart phone, and it can get a signal, you should be able to simply call someone and let them know you're lost and need assistance. Also, most smart phones have a built-in compass, which *should* be able to help you regain your sense of direction.

Another mistake that has sometimes been made by lone adults is that they panic when they realize they've gotten themselves turned around and lost, and they will actually set down their pack (with all their gear), and run off wildly trying to find the road that they know is just beyond the edge of the forest—except, they don't find that forest edge and they keep running, and they never find that pack again. Remember, if lost, STOP! Hug that tree and take stock of the situation.

Children and adults do different things

Adults seem to travel to higher ground when lost, probably in an attempt to find higher ground and get a view of the situation. Children, on the other hand, do not automatically think so pragmatically. Children will travel in the direction of those areas that seem the most interesting, and this usually means wherever there is water. They will travel downhill to the river, or will head in whatever direction where they think there is the greatest possibility of titillating their short term interest.

Search and Rescue teams know that children and adults will follow different patterns when lost—even in the same terrain. They will use this knowledge to hopefully find lost and confused hikers.

What to carry anytime you go hiking

Yes, we've all heard the mantra: the more you know, the less you carry! So why do so many of us continually collect more and more junk that we try to stuff into that very finite pack we carry?

It's one of life's mysteries.

Still, it's true, the more you know, the less you carry, because you know how to avoid trouble in the first place. You have the skills to make fire if you had to, and you know how to use that compass you carry. You know how to make things from wood, so that little pocketknife you carry can really come in handy.

And make sure that what you think you know is actually so! Remember, we learned about many "old husbands' tales" in this book: moss grows on the north sides of trees, all rivers lead to cities, the north star is the brightest star in the sky—that sort of useless "knowledge."

Learn how to do actual things, and learn to use the tools you carry. Also, it's very important that you devise your own everyday survival kit. No one knows your particular needs like you do!

Here are suggestions for the types of things you should never venture into unknown areas without:

The Holy Trinity

Always carry a knife, firestarter, and cordage (of some sort). These three tools can help provide for all your needs.

The "Holy Trinity" includes a knife, a way to make a fire, and cordage. Here we see parachute cord, a Bic lighter and a magnesium fire starter, and a Swiss Army knife.

Categories of items that you should consider carrying:

- Navigation: Map, compass.
- Sun Protection: Hat, sunglasses, lip balm, bandana, etc.
- Insulation: Clothing, space blanket, etc.
- Illumination: Flashlight, candles.
- Fire: Butane lighter, magnesium firestarter, matches.
- First aid: There are many portable kits available. Choose one that meets your needs.
- Tools/repair: Swiss army knife, Leatherman, duct tape, eyeglass repair kit, paracord, twine, etc.
- Nutrition: Food, dry soup, tea, especially things that last.
- Water purification: Water container, water filter, purification pills, a water key, etc.
- Signaling: A whistle, signaling mirror, and a way to call for help such as Resqlink, Spot, or InReach. These devices are reliable even when there is no cell service available.
- Other. Anything else that you personally should carry, like, perhaps, extra cash.

Francisco Loaiza shows some of the gear that he typically carries into the wilderness, especially in his capacity as a Boy Scout leader.

Nicole Deweese shows some basic gear that can be carried in a small backpack. Everyone's choice of gear is different, depending on their experience, location, time of year, etc.

Army veteran Mark Tsunokai likes to be prepared. He shows the gear that he can pack into his North Face day pack to supply his needs for a week or more.

So, should you *always* carry a compass? Some hikers do, some don't. Remember that a map is more important than the compass since it tells you so many things that you couldn't possibly know otherwise. And there are many ways to navigate terrain, as we discussed in Chapter Two, that don't require a map or a compass.

One morning, before our group set out on a day-long hike, one of the members of our group pulled out his latest acquisition. Dwayne showed us his new compass, complete with all the bells and whistles, meaning, it had a fold-up sighting line (like a rifle sight), mirrors, and lots of extras that folded and rotated.

"So, you know how to use it, don't you?" I asked.

"I have no idea," laughed Dwayne, to an eruption of laughter from the group.

Though I presume that Dwayne eventually learned how to use the devise, I told him that for the money he overspent on the compass, he could have had a very enjoyable evening with his wife at a quality restaurant, whereas his new toy compass would likely get minimal use.

QUIZ:

1. Describe the Holy Trinity (that is, the "holy trinity" as defined by the author of this book).
2. A tree-hugger is someone who is part of a nature-worshipping cult. True or False?
3. You're lost and you've decided to leave a note at your temporary camp, in case someone comes. You don't have a paper and pen. How can you leave a more permanent note using common trash?

ANSWERS

1. Knife, fire-starter, cordage.
2. False (though it could be true *some of the time).* You hug a tree if you are lost, meaning, stay put.
3. Write a message on a piece of aluminum from a discarded cola can and hang it in a tree.

TEST YOUR KNOWLEDGE

THE MAP

1. State what can you do with a map alone? (i.e., no compass)
2. State one way in which you can align your map with the natural terrain (without a compass).
3. What direction is almost always at the top of maps?
4. The most useful map for wilderness travel is the _______ map. Briefly describe this type of map.
5. What do the parallel lines on topographical maps represent?
6. State how it is possible to properly align a standard topographical map using the North Star.
7. Look at a topographical map. Identify at least ten symbols (e.g. different types of roads, waterways, fixed objects, etc.).
8. Briefly state how you would draw a fairly accurate map for others to use. (Consider the necessity of maps during survival situations or war situations.)

THE COMPASS

9. The magnetic end of your compass points to
   - South
   - Magnetic South
   - True North
   - Magnetic North
10. Does the magnetic end of a compass dial point to the Earth's North Pole?
11. What is the name for the difference between the True North and Magnetic North?
12. How is this difference (question 11) determined?

13. How does one adjust one's compass to compensate for declination?
14. The compass, as a circle, is divided into _______ degrees.
15. On your compass dial, north is at _______ degrees or _______ degrees.
16. On your compass dial, east is at _______ degrees, south is at _______, and west is at _______ degrees.
17. What can you do with your orienteering compass alone (i.e., without a map)? Briefly state:
    1. ____
    2. ____
18. ☐ TRUE ☐ FALSE: A compass is significantly less useful without a map. A map and a compass should be considered as a team.
19. A compass is carried in the wilderness because (choose):
    - It tells us where we are;
    - It prevents us from getting lost;
    - Everyone says we should carry one;
    - It can double as a fire-starter;
    - It helps us maintain a sense of direction;
    - A map is far more useful with one; and/or
    - It impresses our friends.
20. What part of your clothing/accessories now on your body can be used as a compass? State how to use said item for a compass.

MAP AND COMPASS

21. What can be done with a map and a compass that can't be done with a compass alone?

    1. _________________
    2. _________________
    3. _________________
    4. _________________

5. ___________________
6. ___________________

STARS

22. The diagram below illustrates the constellations of the Big Dipper, Little Dipper, and Cassiopeia. Label the stars (including the North Star) and state how these can be used for direction-finding.

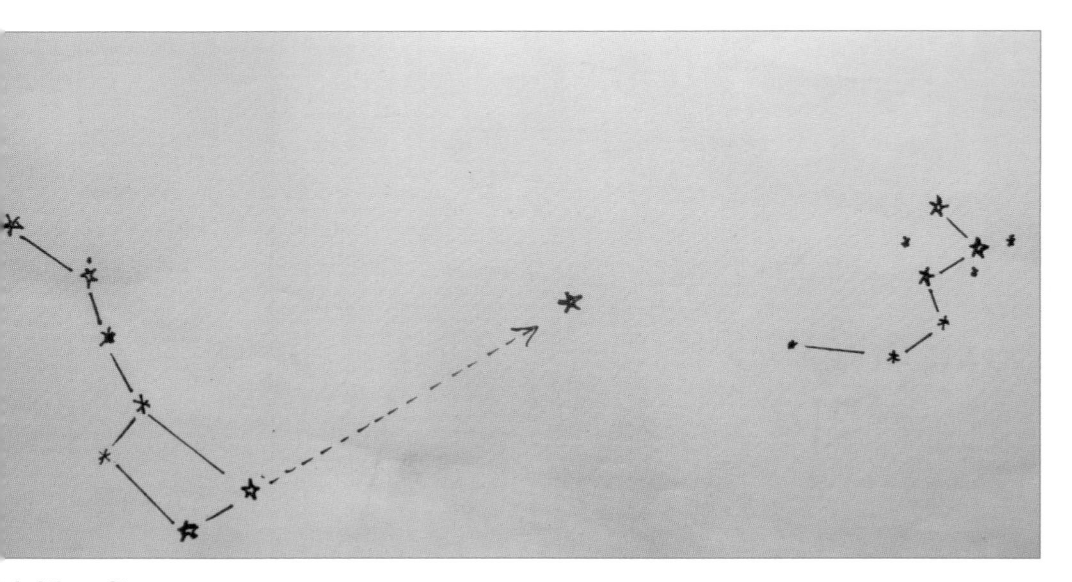

abel these Stars.

23. The diagram here illustrates Orion. Tell how it can be used for direction-finding.

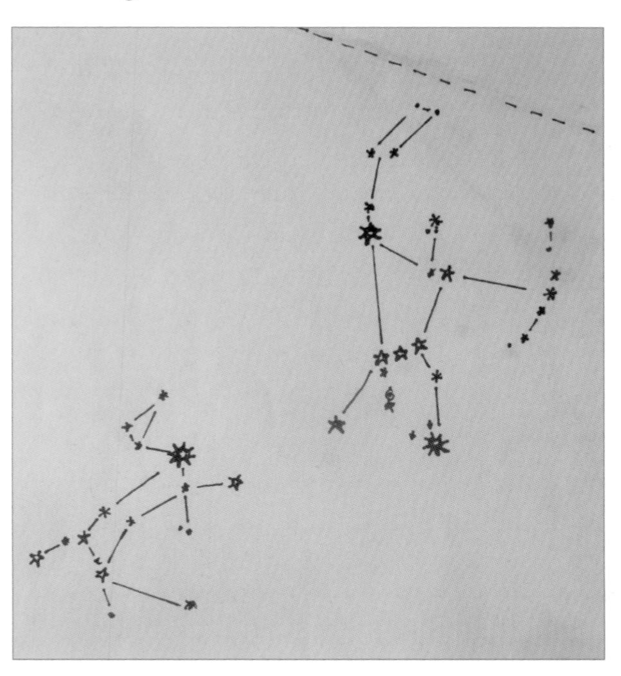

Orion.

24. When you observe the night sky for a period of time, you'll notice that all stars appear to rotate
    - Clockwise
    - Counterclockwise around ___________.
25. Based on the last question, if the Big Dipper/Cassiopeia were not visible, then one could still roughly ascertain direction at night by sighting a single star over the top of two sticks. As you observe a single star, it will appear to move in a particular direction. That direction of movement will tell you which direction you are facing. Draw lines to the correct answers:

    If you are facing . . . . . . the star will appear to

east	rise
west	fall
north	swing flat toward your left
south	swing flat toward your right

A SOLAR CLOCK AND/OR COMPASS

26. If you place a stick in the ground upright at noon in the northern hemisphere, the shadow will be on what side of the stick?
27. In the morning, the shadow from the same stick would be pointing in what direction?
28. In the evening, the shadow from the same stick would be pointing in what direction?
29. Based on the above question, describe how a simple solar clock-compass can be constructed with sticks. Draw an illustration.

NATURAL OBSERVATIONS

30. ☐ TRUE ☐ FALSE: Moss always grows on the north sides of trees.
31. Why would moss grow on the north side of a tree?
32. ☐ TRUE ☐ FALSE: Spider nests usually face south.
33. ☐ TRUE ☐ FALSE: Woodpecker holes are often on the east sides of trees.
34. ☐ TRUE ☐ FALSE: Tips of pines and hemlocks often point east.
35. ☐ TRUE ☐ FALSE: Tips of willows, poplars, and alders often point south.
36. ☐ TRUE ☐ FALSE: Flowers often face south.
37. Why would certain animals and plants face south?
38. How would it be possible to tell directions (generally) by the moistness or dryness of a hillside?
39. If you want to make the least amount of noise, on what side of a hillside should you be? Why?
40. There is a way to tell time (approximately) with the hands alone. How is this done?

ANSWERS

The Map

1. You can gain general and specific information about the environment. The map shows you the roads, trails, significant buildings, waterways, springs, and it indicates elevation. If you can pinpoint your location on the map, and if you can locate one or two other significant landmarks, you can then align the map so that it corresponds with the natural terrain.
2. Lay the map on a flat surface. Ideally, you'll be at a location where you have a view of your surrounding terrain. If you see a water tower on your map, for example, and you can see that actual water tower on the ridge east of you, turn the map until your location and the water tower's location on the map are identical with the actual field conditions.
3. True North.
4. Topographical maps. These maps—which are the symbolic equivalent of an aerial photograph—show the elevation of the land by means of contour lines. Topographical maps also show all significant buildings, waterways, roads, and other landmarks. These are produced by the US Geological Survey.
5. Elevation rise or gain is depicted by parallel lines. If these lines are very close, the elevation is steep. Where the lines are far apart, the land is nearly flat. Also, when you travel "within the lines," you are choosing a level path. When your path crosses these lines, you are rising or falling in elevation.
6. The North Star is only one degree off of True North. Thus, you can locate True North by sighting the North Star at night, and then align your map in that direction.
7. *Teachers need to work with students on this one.*
8. *Teachers need to work with students on this one.*

THE COMPASS

9. Magnetic North.
10. No. The magnetic end of a compass needle points to the Magnetic North pole—which is not a fixed point and which changes slightly from year to year. The Magnetic North pole is not at the same location as the True North pole, which is the point of the earth's axis of rotation.
11. Declination.
12. You must look at the data printed on your map to find the declination for any given area.
13. The simplest way to describe this is that you must adjust your orienteering compass so that the magnetic needle is in alignment with the Magnetic North, as designated on the map. This is most easily done by laying the compass onto the map (which is lying flat), and then turning the map until the compass needle is aligned with the Magnetic North indication on the map.
14. 360 degrees.
15. 0 or 360.
16. East is 90, South is 180, West is 270.
17. Though the usefulness of the compass is limited if you don't have a map, you can determine the cardinal directions of north, south, east, and west. You can also walk in a straight line and return the way you came. You can also practice the PAUL method, as described in this book.
18. True.
19. The best responses are "It helps us maintain a sense of direction," and "A map is far more useful with one." If your orienteering compass has a magnifying glass, it *could* be used as a fire-starter, though I'd not depend on my compass as a fire-starter. A compass does *not* "tell us where we are," and it does *not* "prevent us from getting lost." Those are things that we must do ourselves,

using the compass as a tool. Unfortunately, too many people buy a compass because "everyone says we should carry one." Even more alarming are those who carry a compass because "it impresses our friends."

20. Obviously, you should carry a small compass in your pack or purse, and most cell phones have built-in compasses. However, lacking that, a small needle or pin (maybe a hat pin?) can be magnetized by stroking them with some knives. Magnetized objects can be coated with wax or grease, and floated. One end will point north. All things considered, it's probably easier and more accurate to make a sundial-sun clock with a stick and shadow, or find north with the North Star.

MAP AND COMPASS

21. Here are some possibilities:
    Find the shortest route to some point.
    Find the easiest route around a mountain.
    Chart a course to an unseen destination.
    Find the route from one point to another which allows you to stay on the highest terrain.
    Choose a route which avoids as much contact with "civilization" as possible.
    Go directly to the nearest water sources.
    Go directly to a particular structure.
22. Once you locate the North Star, east is to your right, south behind you, and west to your left. The North Star is sighted by first locating the two "end stars" of the Big Dipper.
23. Orion rises in the east and sets in the west. The imaginary line drawn through Orion is roughly an east-west line.

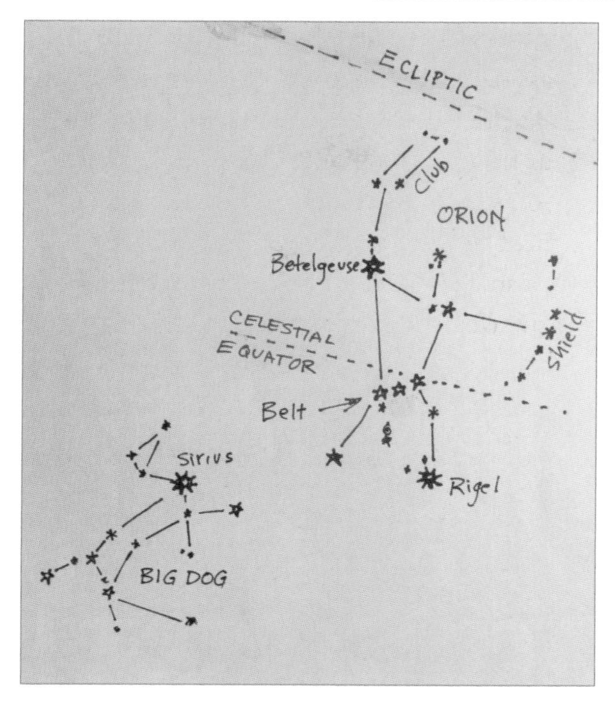

Orion travels just below the ecliptic (in the Northern Hemisphere). Orion "travels" along the Celestial Equator, meaning that it rises in the east and sets in the west.

24. All stars in the northern hemisphere appear to rotate counter-clockwise around the North Star (Polaris).
25. East → rise. West → fall. North → swing flat toward your left. South → swing flat toward your right. The only exception would be if you happened to be sighting a star *under* the North Star, in which case it would be moving to your right.

A SOLAR CLOCK AND/OR COMPASS

26. To the north.
27. West
28. East.
29. See Sun Compass image page 29.

NATURAL OBSERVATIONS

30. False. Moss will grow on all sides of trees, as long as there is moisture and shade.
31. The north sides of houses, hills, trees, fences, etc. remain in the shade much of the time, and thus retain more moisture.
32. True. Note the word "usually"—not "always."
33. False. Woodpeckers will peck wherever they can find insects. However, the pileated woodpecker *tends* to peck primarily on the east sides of trees.
34. True, probably due to prevailing winds. Note the word "often"—not "always."
35. True, probably because these trees are often growing in waterways and canyons with prevailing down-canyon winds at night. Note the word "often"—not "always."
36. True.
37. To face the warmth of the sun.
38. Hills which run in an east-west direction will have greener vegetation because of more retained moisture on the north side. The south exposed side will tend to be drier, and will probably also have different plant communities due to the constant exposure to the sun.
39. The south side would be generally noisier due to the presence of dry twigs and other dry material. The north side, with more moisture, will tend to be less noisy to walk through.
40. See Chapter Two: The Sun, under The Setting Sun, page 35 for these details.

APPENDIX

HOW TO MAKE A SIMPLE STAR DIAL FOR TELLING TIME

When I took astronomy classes in college, we were taught many ways to read the stars, and to determine time or direction from their location. Remember, all the stars appear to rotate counter-clockwise around Polaris because of the earth's rotation.

If you have a fixed site to observe stars—such as two stakes driven into the ground where you site over them, or at a fixed location where you site a distant peak—you will observe that a given star will return to the very exact site of the first observation in exactly twenty-three hours, fifty-six minutes, and 4.09 seconds. This is the period of time

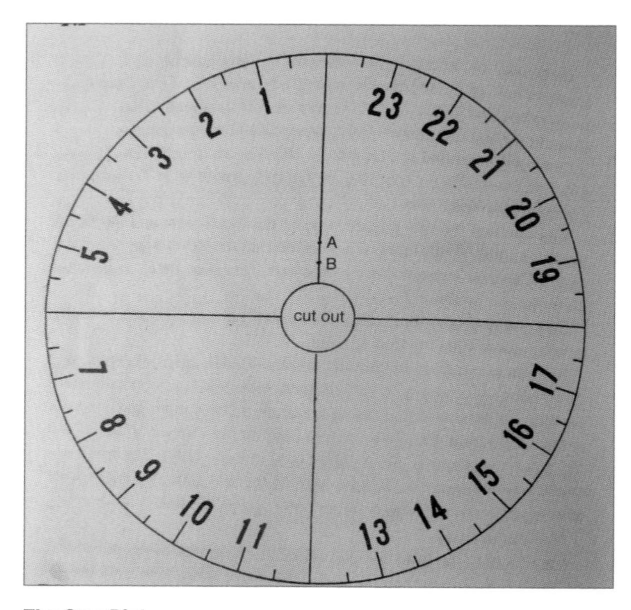

The Star Dial.

known as the sidereal day. It almost corresponds to the average solar day of twenty-four hours.

Our astronomy professor had us photocopy and cut out the round dial that is reprinted in this book. We brought this along on our field trips and used it to tell time by the location of the stars.

So first, photocopy the dial in this book onto heavy paper, or just copy on regular paper and then mount it on heavy cardboard. I recommend that you enlarge it so that it's at least about 8 inches in diameter. Cut it out so you have a round dial, and cut out the center hole.

At the points marked A and B, punch holes and tie a cord to the holes, so that the cord hangs below the edge of the dial. Attach a weight at the end of the cord so this serves like a plumb line.

Now your dial is done.

In order to use this dial for time-telling, you have to be able to identify the North Star, and the constellations of the Big Dipper and Cassiopeia.

James Ruther examines the Star Dial which has been mounted on stiff cardboard. Note the center hole has been cut out, and there is a key at the end of the string for a weight. To use properly, the string must be aligned with the "12" at the bottom of the dial, with "24" at the top.

At night time, the Star Dial is held up to the sky so that the North Star is viewed in the middle hole. Then, you locate the position of Beta Cassiopeiae on the edge of the Star Dial.

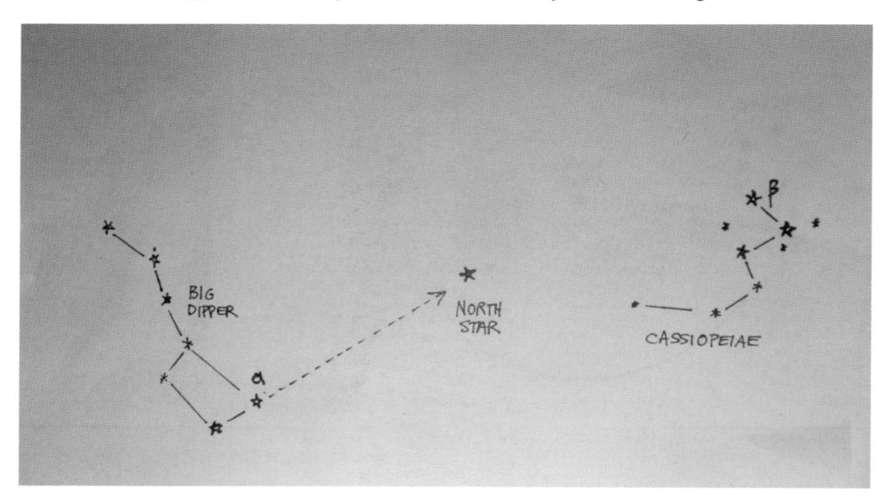

With the North Star in the middle of the Star Dial, you then locate Beta Cassiopeiae. See text for details.

When I was an astronomy student, we always carried flashlights with a red lens because we could still see our paperwork with the red lens, but our eyes did not have to constantly adjust from a bright light and back to the stars. So bring a red lens flashlight with you when you go into the outdoors.

On a clear night, find a spot where you have an unobstructed view of the northern horizon. If you're too close to the city, you won't be able to see any but the brightest stars.

You've already learned how to identify the North Star, the Big Dipper, and Cassiopeia. If you're uncertain, refer back to the illustrations given here.

We know that the two pointer stars of the Big Dipper and the North Star lie on a line. If this line is extended beyond the North Star, one of the stars of Cassiopeia comes close to the line. This star, Beta Cassiopeiae, misses the line by about 15 degrees.

On a clear night, hold the dial with the numerals facing you so that the North Star (Polaris) can be seen in the center of the hole. Turn the dial so that the plumb line lies along the line from the central hole to the numeral 12.

Hold your star dial at such a distance so that Beta Cassiopeiae appears just on the edge of the dial. Make sure the North Star remains in the middle hole of your dial. Now read the position of Beta Cassiopeiae, approximating as closely as possible the fraction of the hour. This reading is the hour angle of Beta Cassiopeiae, also termed the local sidereal time.

Now the math begins, and we will convert the sidereal time into standard time.

At around March 21 each year, the sun is at the vernal equinox and its right ascension is zero hours. (Right Ascension corresponds roughly to the longitude lines on the earth's surface, and it is measured in hours, minutes, and seconds.) The daily average change in the right ascension is just about four minutes per day, or two hours per month.

Therefore, the right ascension is easiest figured by adding four minutes per day for each day that has elapsed between March 21 and the date of your observation. Subtract the right ascension from the observed sidereal time. This gives you the hour angle of the mean sun.

Thus, **Sidereal Time - Right Ascension = Hour Angle.**

Next, add 12 in order to obtain the local civil time. This is because the hour angle tells us how many hours have elapsed since noon, but civil time is reckoned from midnight. **Hour Angle + 12 = Local Civil Time.**

Next, you must correct for the longitude from where you are observing in order to obtain standard time. To make this correction, you first need to know two things:

1. The precise longitude of your observation; and
2. The precise longitude of the standard for your time zone.

The first is obtained by checking a topographical map of your area, or by calling a map shop or local geologist.

The second is also simple; refer to the chart below:

TIME ZONE	STANDARD
Pacific	120 W.
Mountain	105 W.
Central	90 W.
Eastern	75 W.
Atlantic	60 W.

To obtain your longitude correction, you need to figure the difference between your time zone standard and your point of observation. Since each degree represents four minutes of time, you multiply your difference by four. This gives you your correction.

If you are observing east of your time standard meridian, you must **subtract** the correction from the local civil time. If you are observing west of your time standard, you must **add** the correction to the local civil time.

So let's summarize the formula:

East: Local Civil Time - Correction = Standard Time.

West: Local Civil Time + Correction = Standard Time.

It's likely that most of your observations will be made at one location, so you won't need to refigure this last one over and over again.

Finally, you subtract one hour if you are currently operating under Daylight Savings Time.

That's it!

If each concept described here has been clearly understood, you now should be able to accurately obtain the correct time from the stars.

It may happen that you cannot see Beta Cassiopeiae. In such case, you can use Alpha Ursae Majoris (the Big Dipper) as your reference star. In this case, the sidereal time will be the reading on your dial plus eleven hours.

At times when I couldn't see Beta Cassiopeiae, I've fairly accurately estimated its position. By observing Alpha Ursae Majoris, I was able to determine—with near accuracy—the position of where I knew Beta Cassiopeiae had to be.

The following summary is for your ready-reference:

Step 1: Sidereal Time - Right Ascension = Hour Angle.
Step 2: Hour Angle + 12 = Local Civil Time.
Step 3: East: Local Civil Time - Correction = Standard Time.
West: Local Civil Time + Correction = Standard Time.
Step 4: (If Daylight Saving Time):
Standard Time - 1 hour = Daylight Saving Time.

Now, let's use an example to clarify all of the foregoing points.

I am at home in Northeastern Los Angeles. The date is June 21. I go outdoors, locate the North Star, and I position my star dial so that the North Star is in the dial's middle hole. I make certain that the dial is properly aligned so that 24 is at the top and 12 at the bottom. Next, I locate Beta Cassiopeiae and position the star dial so that Beta Cassiopeiae is observed just at the edge of the dial. I observe Beta Cassiopeiae at 17½ on the dial. I can now put the star dial away and do some figuring.

First, I figure the right ascension. June 21 is exactly three months from the vernal equinox (March 21), and so the right ascension is easily figured: At two hours per month, the right ascension equals six hours. I subtract 6 from the 17½ reading and I get 11½.

Now I add 12 and I get 23½, or 11:30 p.m.

As stated earlier, the standard meridian for the Pacific Time Zone is the 120th meridian. I live at 118" 12', which is east of the standard. The difference between 120 and 118" 12' is 1 degree 48'. Since each degree corresponds to four minutes of time, I multiply this difference by four, which equals 7 minutes and 12 seconds.

As indicated in Step 3, this correction is subtracted from the local civil time. Thus, 11:30 p.m. minus 7 minutes 12 seconds give us roughly 11:23 p.m.

Finally, I subtract another hour since Daylight Saving Time is in use on the date of my observation. The time then is 10:23 p.m.

I look at my watch and I see that I'm six minutes off. Where did I go wrong? When I get home, I check the time and learn that my watch was three minutes off, leaving me with an observational error of three minutes. That not's bad!

With a bit of practice, you'll be able to figure time this way in about a minute or so.

REFERENCES

The Natural Navigator: The Rediscovered Art of Letting Nature be Your Guide, by Tristan Gooley, The Experiment, 2010. If you enjoy learning how to navigate by common-sense observational skills, you must read this book!

The Stars: A New Way to See Them, by H. A. Rey, Houghton Mifflin Co., Boston, 1976. (Originally published 1952). This is the best way to learn to recognize the constellations and understand the night sky that I've ever seen in print.

Be Expert with Map and Compass: The Complete Orienteering Handbook, by Björn Kjellström, Macmillan, 1994. (Originally published 1955). A step by step approach to orienteering, the art of using a map and compass, along with many exercises. This classic is the only book you'll need on the intricacies of using a map and compass.

The Green Beret's Compass Course, by Don Paul, 2006. This is the long version of the PAUL system described in this book.

Constellations of the Northern Sky, Mechler and Chartrand, National Audubon Society Pocket Guide, Knopf, 1998.

The Stones of Time: Calendars, Sundials, and Stone Chambers of Ancient Ireland, by Martin Brennan, Inner Traditions International, Rochester,

VT, 1994. Demonstrates that ancient man knew how to accurately record the path of the sun and moon.

Earth Magic: The Astounding Mystery of the Greatest of all Lost Civilizations, by Francis Hitching. William Morrow and Company, 1977. Hitching examines the archaeological remains of ancient man of 5000 years ago, and more, to demonstrate that the knowledge of equinoxes, solstices, eclipses, cycles of the moon, etc., were well-known to these ancient builders.

Testing Your Outdoor Survival Skills, by Christopher Nyerges, Survival News Service, 1994.

How to Survive Anywhere by Christopher Nyerges, Stackpole, includes a short section on navigation.

Sundials: History, Theory, and Practice, by René R. J. Rohr, Dover Publications, 1970.

Sundials: Their Construction and Use by R. Newton Mayall and Margaret W. Mayall, Dover Publications, 2000.

Sundials: Their Theory and Construction by Albert Waugh, Dover Publications, 1973.

Easy-to-Make Wooden Sundials by Milton Stoneman, Dover Publications, 1982.

Ron Hood's "Navigation" video [volume 4 of his WoodMaster's series] from www.Survival.com.

Source of compasses and signaling devices: www.survivalresources.com

INDEX